Quantifying Potential Cost Avoidance Implications of Outcomes Reported in Behavioral and Social Science Research

BRUCE R. ORVIS, HEATHER KRULL, MICHAEL G. SHANLEY

Prepared for the United States Army
Approved for public release; distribution unlimited

RAND ARROYO CENTER

For more information on this publication, visit **www.rand.org/t/RRA1303-1**.

About RAND

The RAND Corporation is a research organization that develops solutions to public policy challenges to help make communities throughout the world safer and more secure, healthier and more prosperous. RAND is nonprofit, nonpartisan, and committed to the public interest. To learn more about RAND, visit www.rand.org.

Research Integrity

Our mission to help improve policy and decisionmaking through research and analysis is enabled through our core values of quality and objectivity and our unwavering commitment to the highest level of integrity and ethical behavior. To help ensure our research and analysis are rigorous, objective, and nonpartisan, we subject our research publications to a robust and exacting quality-assurance process; avoid both the appearance and reality of financial and other conflicts of interest through staff training, project screening, and a policy of mandatory disclosure; and pursue transparency in our research engagements through our commitment to the open publication of our research findings and recommendations, disclosure of the source of funding of published research, and policies to ensure intellectual independence. For more information, visit www.rand.org/about/research-integrity.

RAND's publications do not necessarily reflect the opinions of its research clients and sponsors.

Published by the RAND Corporation, Santa Monica, Calif.

Library of Congress Cataloging-in-Publication Data is available for this publication.

ISBN: 978-1-9774-1086-3

About This Report

This report documents research and analysis conducted as part of two projects entitled *Quantifying the Value of Behavioral* and *Social Science Research* and *Quantifying the Value of Behavioral and Social Science Research Follow-On*, both sponsored by the U.S. Army Research Institute for the Behavioral and Social Sciences. The purpose of the first project was to develop utility functions that translate the incremental effects of outcome criteria often used in behavioral and social science research results into estimates of the value of those changes, such as cost avoidance or other benefits. The purpose of the second project was to continue and expand on the work of the first project.

This research was conducted within RAND Arroyo Center's Personnel, Training, and Health Program. RAND Arroyo Center, part of the RAND Corporation, is a federally funded research and development center (FFRDC) sponsored by the United States Army.

RAND operates under a "Federal-Wide Assurance" (FWA00003425) and complies with the *Code of Federal Regulations for the Protection of Human Subjects Under United States Law* (45 CFR 46), also known as "the Common Rule," as well as with the implementation guidance set forth in DoD Instruction 3216.02. As applicable, this compliance includes reviews and approvals by RAND's Institutional Review Board (the Human Subjects Protection Committee) and by the U.S. Army. The views of sources utilized in this study are solely their own and do not represent the official policy or position of DoD or the U.S. Government.

Acknowledgments

We appreciate the guidance that we received throughout the two projects from our project monitors, Tonia Heffner, Gerald (Jay) Goodwin, and Len White, of the U.S. Army Research Institute for the Behavioral and Social Sciences. We are grateful to COL Robert Montz at the Office of the Surgeon General for data he supplied for our analysis. We want to acknowledge the important contributions of our current and former RAND colleagues, Christopher Maerzluft, Andrew Naber, Joachin Rubalcaba, Cameron Wright, and Blake Cignarella, who provided earlier drafts of many of the study write-ups and made methodological contributions. We also wish to thank Anita Szafran, Jaime Hastings, Laurie McDonald, Matt Cefalu, James Hosek, and Michael Mattock for providing research support, data analysis, or other inputs to our analysis. Finally, we thank Lionel Galway at RAND and Matthew Goldberg at Institute for Defense Analyses for their thoughtful reviews of the draft. Their comments and feedback helped improve this report.

Summary

Senior leaders often broadly appreciate the relevance of behavioral and social science research but are not able to readily compare the value of screening tests, interventions, or other factors analyzed in this literature with the benefits of operational programs or of tools to address different sets of outcomes. The research summarized in this report translates changes in outcomes often reported in behavioral and social science research results into potential cost avoidance estimates and other benefits valued by senior leaders. We focused on specific outcomes in the behavioral and social science literature of interest to the project sponsor and personnel managers: initial training attrition; first-term attrition; reenlistment and retention; job qualification; recruit market expansion; training effectiveness; recruiting resource costs and productivity; legal incidents; injuries; suicide; and health care costs, utilization, and outcomes. The types of factors we investigated included personality tests and screeners, additional screeners, incentives, compensation, recruiting resource allocation, deployments, telemedicine, and distance learning versus classroom training.

At the request of the sponsor, we focused primarily on estimating the potential annual costs avoided for each of the studies selected within the outcome and study factor areas. In developing and applying utility functions, we used recent Army data and estimated potential costs avoided for each study independently of other research. We considered reduction of certain serious legal incidents and fewer suicides as valuable in their own right and, therefore, did not do a cost analysis for these outcomes.

Ideally, research should report results that can be directly used to estimate the effect of a screener or other intervention on the outcome of interest, such as a complete set of regression-based results or actual results for categorical predictors. For researchers interested in maximizing the extent to which their work can be interpreted by and for policymakers, we recommend providing these data in future work. However, while many of the studies we summarize in this report provide all the necessary data, others do not. As the report demonstrates, methods are available in some of these cases that allow us to approximate the effect on the outcome. These methods should be considered a less-preferable backup.

Furthermore, while we found evidence of the success of certain factors in reducing other legal incidents or adverse medical outcomes, we were unable to identify available associated cost measures. Additional research in these areas would be useful to quantify the financial benefits of screener(s), intervention(s), or other factor(s) that reduce the frequency of these outcomes.

Contents

Tables

Chapter 1. Introduction

The research summarized in this report translates changes in many of the numerous types of outcomes reported in behavioral and social science research results, such as attrition, reenlistment, job qualification, injury rates, training costs, and health care costs, into estimates of the value of the changes, such as potential cost avoidance or other benefits, that can enable senior leaders to compare results across different types of interventions and be considered in funding decisions. Senior leaders often broadly appreciate the relevance of research but are not able to readily compare the value of interventions analyzed in this literature with the benefits of operational programs or of tools to address different sets of outcomes. In an increasingly constrained fiscal environment, these tools can help senior leaders make informed decisions about how to allocate scarce resources across a variety of operational programs and interventions. Making behavioral and social science research tangibly useful in this way could also help inform decisionmakers about the value of resourcing research generally.

To develop these tools, it is necessary to identify the types of benefits in which senior leaders have the most interest, develop metrics for these benefits, identify the data needed to quantify the benefits using these metrics, and develop the methodology to translate the incremental effects of changes in outcome criteria into estimates of the benefits. Such outcomes, for example, could involve reduced attrition at various points in recruiting and commissioning, training, or during time serving in units; improved retention; disciplinary incident reduction; or improvements in soldier health and well-being.

Research Approach

The initial step in the research was to identify potential focus areas and metrics. We worked closely with the sponsor to identify broad focus areas of research outcomes and benefit metrics of interest to the U.S. Army on which the project should focus. Within these focus areas, in coordination with the sponsor, we also identified potential effects of improvements in these outcomes that could result from behavioral and social science research. Preliminary prioritization of these areas and metrics considered such factors as importance for Army leaders and immediacy of application and use of the metrics.

Starting with the broad focus areas identified in the first step, we conducted an extensive literature review to identify the range of outcome criteria commonly used in behavioral and social science research and perspectives on the appropriate benefit metrics for these outcomes. The review led to inclusion of a number of broad areas, such as attrition, retention, job qualification, and health outcomes. We identified 50 to 150 articles in each area. We reviewed each article to identify the independent variables and the outcomes. We discarded studies of variables or outcomes not relevant to the Army. We then categorized the remaining studies by types of outcomes and interventions assessed.

We reviewed details of the factor(s) studied and related outcome(s) for each study that potentially covered outcomes, areas, and benefits approved in our earlier meetings with the sponsor. We then assessed the types of information needed to translate the outcome results into quantifiable levels of the benefits, their sources, the feasibility of accessing them, and the analytical difficulty of generating the benefit estimates. Among the studies that were feasible to analyze, we gave greater priority to those that had interventions and outcomes that were related to those in other studies, to support generalizability across the interventions reviewed. The retained studies cover the following outcomes and interventions:

- outcomes
    - initial training attrition
    - first-term attrition
    - reenlistment
    - job qualification
    - recruit market expansion
    - training effectiveness
    - recruiting resource costs and productivity
    - legal incidents
    - injuries
    - suicide
    - health care costs
    - health care utilization
    - health care outcomes
- factors studied
    - personality test or screener
    - additional screeners
    - incentives
    - compensation
    - recruiting resource allocation
    - deployment
    - telemedicine
    - distance learning versus classroom
    - other programs and interventions.

Using the prioritized outcomes and benefit metrics, we developed utility functions that translate outcomes reported in behavior and social science research into estimates of potential cost avoidance or other benefits. For example, for many screening measures, we estimated the potential effect of eliminating the lowest 10 percent of scorers on reducing attrition, increasing retention, and on related cost avoidance. In other cases, we estimated the effect of training programs in reducing injuries or increasing graduation rates. In others, we estimated potential cost avoidance from converting portions of classroom training programs to distance or computerized training. Chapter 2 discusses our methodology in detail.

This report documents the studies assessed, the outcomes they reported, their logical linkages to the benefits identified, utility function development and methodology to make the linkages, and our accompanying analyses and results in applying the methodology to the data reported in the studies. In the final chapter, the report also discusses areas where further research and analysis could be useful in estimating potential benefits for additional intervention-outcome pairs.

Organization of Report

Chapter 2 discusses common language, methodology, data, and formulas used throughout the report. Chapter 3 discusses research pertaining to initial training attrition. In Chapter 4, we consider attrition throughout the first term. Reenlistment and retention research is discussed in Chapter 5. Chapter 6 follows with a discussion of research on job qualification, training effectiveness, recruiting resource costs, recruiter productivity, and legal issues. In Chapter 7, we consider research on injuries, suicide, and health care. Chapter 8 provides a review of our analyses and results and their implications, as well as considerations for further research. Appendix A discusses inputs to our calculations. Last, Appendix B shows the derivation of our Special Forces (SF)–related training cost metrics.

Chapter 2. Selected Methodologies and Data Used Throughout This Report

In this chapter, we describe methodologies and data sources that are used for multiple studies discussed throughout this report. We begin with a discussion of which studies were included, that is, which types of studies were included as being relevant to the Army and which were excluded.

Study Inclusion Criteria

We reviewed four different types of studies:[1]

- studies of U.S. Army populations
- studies of other U.S. military populations
- studies of other countries' military populations
- studies of nonmilitary populations.

We considered studies of U.S. Army populations to be relevant provided that the screening measures they used are still in use or could be used. We considered studies of other U.S. military populations to be relevant provided that the outcome measure also applied to the Army. For example, the Army has fixed-wing pilots and navigators, and we applied results from an Air Force study on success in pilot and navigator training and adjusted the number of total trainee hours to account for the number of Army pilots and navigators relative to the Air Force.[2]

For the last two categories, studies of other countries' military populations and studies of nonmilitary populations, we considered results to be relevant provided they met certain criteria:

1. The screening measures they used are still in use by the U.S. Army or could be used.
2. The outcome measure is relevant to the Army.
3. The rate of the outcome is generally consistent with the Army rate.

---

[1] The studies were drawn from searches of the following databases and collections: Academic Search Complete, Army Institute of Public Health, U.S. Army Research Institute for the Behavioral and Social Sciences (ARI), Army Research Institute of Environmental Medicine, Business Source Complete, Center for Naval Analyses, the Cumulative Index to Nursing and Allied Health Literature Plus with Full Text, Criminal Justice Abstracts, Defense Technical Information Center, Military & Government Collection, National Criminal Justice Reference Service Abstracts, Published International Literature on Traumatic Stress, PsycINFO, PubMed, RAND Corporation publications, and Social Sciences Abstracts. The subjects searched included recruiting; attrition; aptitude, cognitive, capability, etc., tests and job performance; training; legal incident reduction; and health care and outcomes. We searched back to the beginning of the all-volunteer force.

[2] For example, see Study 3.14: Air Force Officer Qualifying Test (AFOQT): Predictors of Undergraduate Pilot Training and Undergraduate Navigator Training Success (Arth et al., 1990). Note that Chapters 3 through 7 each begin with a table listing the studies covered and assigning numbers.

For example, we included a study that examined the relationship between psychological screeners and training outcomes among Norwegian sailors. The screeners have been used by the U.S. Army; training completion is a relevant outcome; and the Norwegian outcome rate is generally consistent with the U.S. Army's rate.[3]

Next, we describe the methods used to translate outcomes in these studies to potential costs avoided.

Analytic Approach

The approach we used to convert outcomes from each study into potential costs avoided depended on how the results were reported. In general, studies contained three types of results:

1. regression coefficients, odds ratios, or hazard and risk ratios
2. reported or regression-based categorical classifications
3. correlations or multiple regression results.[4]

In the following subsections, we discuss our approach for each type of study, which varied in some respects, depending on the specific outcome.

Studies That Reported Regression Coefficients, Odds Ratios, or Hazard/Risk Ratios

If a study used regression analysis, results were typically reported as regression coefficients, odds ratios, or hazard/risk ratios. In some cases, the study used categorical screening measures in lieu of psychological tests. If the outcome was a change in attrition, we calculated the difference in the attrition rate between those who were treated by the intervention and those who were not. We applied the regression results together with information on the distribution of scores when reported for the predictor variable (or assumed it to be normally distributed) to determine the difference in completion rates. We next computed a revised mean score after dropping the bottom 10 percent of screener scores (essentially assuming that the information provided by the study could be used to screen out this subpopulation).[5] Using the estimated reduction in attrition, we estimated the associated potential cost avoidance given the cost of a training graduate by multiplying that cost per graduate times the number of potential trainees saved.

---

[3] See Study 3.5: Psychological Measures as Predictors of Military Training Performance (Hartmann et al., 2003) and Rorschach Variables and Big Five Scales as Predictors of Military Training Completion: A Replication Study of the Selection of Candidates to the Naval Special Forces in Norway (Hartmann and Grønnerød, 2009). For an example of a nonmilitary study that met these criteria, see Study 3.4: The "Big Five" Personality Factors in the IPI and MMPI: Predictors of Police Performance (Cortina et al., 1992).

[4] Multiple regression is a statistical technique that uses multiple explanatory variables to predict the outcome for a response variable.

[5] We chose 10 percent because it is the largest percentage of potential enlistees that we wanted to screen out to limit the effect on enlistment supply. For reallocation across quintiles, we do the allocation proportionally to limit the effect on the difference between the demand for each quintile and the supply.

If the outcome of the study was a change in retention, we assumed a normal reenlistment rate of 50 percent (the actual rate at the time of our analysis) and subtracted from it the retention effect reported by the study.[6] We then estimated the Selective Reenlistment Bonus (SRB) that would be needed to achieve the same increase in retention using information from the Dynamic Retention Model (DRM).[7] Potential cost avoidance was then estimated by multiplying the required SRB value by the total number of reenlistees among those reaching the end of their first term (70,000 enlistees multiplied by 0.6525, based on the first-term attrition rate shown in Table 2.1, multiplied by 0.5, the target reenlistment rate).[8]

Table 2.1. First-Term Cumulative Attrition Rates

Months of Service	Attrition Rate
6	11.59
12	15.92
18	19.84
24	23.40
30	26.86
36	30.40
42	32.62
48	36.87
First term	34.75

SOURCE: Author calculations using TAPDB covering FY 2001–FY 2011 accessions.

A special case for retention studies occurs when the outcome reported is retention intentions in lieu of actual retention rates. In such cases, because the outcome reflects reenlistment intentions rather than reenlistment per se, an additional multiplier (0.37) is factored into the calculation to reflect the predicted relationship between reenlistment intentions and actual reenlistment (Campbell and Zook, 1996).

---

[6] The exception was when the study reported the specific reenlistment rate underlying the regression results. In these few cases, we calculated the percentage increase in reenlistment relative to the reported reenlistment rate and used it to calculate the size of the SRB needed to achieve the same increase.

[7] See Table 2.2. For information on the DRM, see Asch, Hosek, and Mattock, 2014; Asch, Mattock, and Hosek, 2013; Asch, Mattock, and Hosek, 2014; Asch et al., 2008; Asch et al., 2016; and Knapp et al., 2016.

[8] For example, see Study 5.6: Impact of the Army Continuing Education System (ACES) on Soldier Retention and Performance: Data Analyses (Sticha et al., 2003).

Studies That Reported Results Based on Categorical Classifications

A second way that studies reported results is based on categorical classifications, such as quintiles of a population. In some cases, studies reported rates directly for the groups; in other cases, studies reported regression-based predictions to place individuals into different categories. In these cases, we removed the bottom 10 percent of recruits (for example, the lowest 10 percent of scorers) and distributed them evenly among the other categories. For example, consider a study that reported attrition rates for high school graduates, youth scoring in the upper half of the Armed Forces Qualification Test (AFQT), or a combination of the two. In such cases, we normally eliminated the bottom 10 percent from a given category and redistributed it to the remaining category (categories).[9]

In the case of quintiles, the top four quintiles end up with 22.5 percent of the population, and 10 percent remain in the bottom quintile. We used these rebalanced quintiles and their associated outcome rates to compare to the original results and multiplied the number of people saved (the number who do not attrit because of their improved placement in the quintiles) by annual throughput and by cost to estimate total cost savings.

As part of RAND Arroyo Center's work on the Recruit Selection Tool (Orvis et al., 2018), we used data from the Total Army Personnel Data Base (TAPDB) covering soldiers who accessed into the Regular Army during fiscal years (FYs) 2001–2011.[10] Using these data, we calculated six-month interval attrition rates (as shown in Table 2.1). Some of these studies directly report Army attrition rates for the measures they were evaluating. In such cases, we used the reported rates in lieu of those in the noted table. Some studies also pertain to specific subpopulations, such as military police (MP), SF, or other particular occupational specialties. In such cases, unless otherwise indicated, we performed our analysis for the number of persons in the specialties and derived separate accession and training costs, as indicated in the study write-ups and appendices.[11]

Studies That Reported Pairwise Correlations or Multiple Correlations

In some studies, only correlations or multiple correlations (Rs) between the predictor or screening measure and the outcome were reported. In such cases, we applied the

---

[9] For example, see Study 3.12: Attrition in the Army from the Signing of the Enlistment Contract Through 180 Days of Service (Fischl and Blackwell, 2000).

[10] See Orvis et al., 2018.

[11] For example, see Study 3.6: Psychological Hardiness Predicts Success in US Army Special Forces Candidates (Bartone et al., 2008).

Brogden-Cronbach-Gleser model to estimate the change in the outcome measure (e.g., attrition or retention rate).[12]

The Brogden-Cronbach-Gleser model for utility analysis has the following formula:

$$\Delta\$Utility = \left[(r_{xy})(N)(Z_x)(SD_y)\$n\right],$$

where

- r_{xy} is the predictor's relationship with the outcome.
- N is the number of outcomes potentially affected by the predictor.
- Zx is a shift in the predictor's standard normal distribution by a chosen percentage which was 10 percent in most cases, as described earlier.
- SDy is the standard deviation of the outcome.
- $\$n$ is a conversion of the outcome measure to dollars per person.

For attrition studies, the following types of information are needed:

- the association between a predictor variable (e.g., personality test) and the outcome of interest (e.g., attrition), or r_{xy},
- the number of people to whom the association and outcome are being applied (e.g., number of accessions).
- the standard deviation of the outcome measure (or information that can be directly used to calculate it, such as the probability of the outcome), or SD_y,
- the cost per person of the outcome.

The first and third measures are multiplied together to generate the *effect size*, which we report in our results table for each study. We then also apply

- the new mean of the standard normal scores of the predictor variable after removing the lowest 10 percent of scorers with the worst outcomes according to the study. The mean standard normal score ("Z-score") then becomes 0.195 (Z_x in the equation).[13]
- the number of persons to whom the predictor measure is applied (e.g., the approximate accession cohort of 70,000 at the time of this project), or N in the equation, and
- the cost per person of the outcome (e.g., applicable recruiting and training costs for replacing a soldier who attrits, estimated as $75,638 on average for each new accession; see Appendix A), or $\$n$ above.

---

[12] See, for example, Boudreau, 1983; Boudreau, 1991; Cascio and Aguinis, 2011; Holling, 1998; Murphy, 1986; and Russell, 2016. As Russell notes, "When X and Y are continuous, it is preferable to use the Brogden-Cronbach-Gleser model instead of the Taylor-Russell model, which assumes a dichotomous outcome measure, avoiding complexities caused by having to use tetrachoric correlations."

[13] The standard normal distribution has a mean value of zero and a standard deviation of one. Normal distributions are commonly used in social science research as the underlying distribution of psychological tests and other independent variables and screening measures. The standard normal distribution for a given normal distribution is generated by subtracting the mean (average) of the scores from the scores and then dividing that value by the standard deviation of the normal scores. See, for example, Johnson and Kotz, 1970, pp. 81–84.

Multiplying these five elements provides the potential costs avoided because of a reduction in the attrition rate.[14]

If the outcome reported in the study was retention, we again started by applying the Brogden-Cronbach-Gleser method. Consider a study in which correlations for two psychological screening surveys were the predictor measures. We screened out the lowest 10 percent of scorers on these measures (again, this shifts the mean of the standard normal distributions for these screening measures from 0.000 to 0.195). As described earlier, we assumed a normal reenlistment rate of 50 percent. The percentage point increase in retention was calculated using the correlation between each of the screening measure scores and retention (0.10 in both cases). Analogously to the procedure described earlier for attrition, here we multiplied the correlation by the standard deviation of the reenlistment rate (i.e., the square root of 0.5 multiplied by 0.5, which equals 0.5) times 0.195, resulting in an estimated increase in the reenlistment rate of 0.975 percentage point.

The estimated increase in the reenlistment rate (0.975 percentage point) is next subtracted from the 50 percent reenlistment rate, yielding 49.025 percent. The magnitude of the proportional reenlistment increase that would be needed to reach 50 percent from 49.025 percent is calculated as 50 / 49.025 – 1 = 1.01989 – 1 = 0.01989, or 1.989 percent. As also discussed, the size of the SRB needed to achieve the same increase is estimated using results from the DRM and then applied to estimate potential costs avoided.[15]

In addition to attrition and retention, we analyzed studies on a variety of other social science outcomes, e.g., savings from computer-based training, improved recruiter productivity, and reduction in injuries from training programs. On occasion, the studies reported results as described earlier (e.g., regressions), and we analyzed these in the same way we did the attrition studies. In most cases, however, they report the outcomes of interest for a population, and we applied those numbers (and the cost of any related programs that generated the savings) in our calculations of potential cost avoided. We describe our methodology in more detail in each of these studies.

Datasets and Databases Used in Our Analyses

Our utility analyses described throughout this report drew on a number of Army data sources. They include the Regular Army Analyst file, a dataset that contains enlistment contract and accession information records for new recruits, and information on attrition, performance, reenlistment, and population sizes (for studies that applied to specific subpopulations, such as MP, SF, or other particular occupational specialties) in the TAPDB, both maintained by the U.S.

---

[14] For example, see Study 4.3: Relations Between Select21 Predictor Measures and First-Term Attrition (Putka and Bradley, 2008).

[15] For example, see Study 5.1: Personality and Success Among Military Enlisted Personnel: An Historical Prospective Study of U.S. Navy Corpsmen (Vickers, Hervig, and Booth, 1996).

Army Human Resources Command. Training performance information was drawn from the Army Training Requirements and Resources System (ATRRS), maintained by Headquarters, Department of the Army (HQDA), Office of Deputy Chief of Staff for Personnel (G-1).

Attrition Rates

As discussed, if a study reported actual attrition rates, we used them in our analysis. However, many studies do not report this information, so we calculated and used a standard set of first-term attrition rates overall and at six-month intervals. These rates were calculated using the TAPDB covering soldiers who accessed into the Regular Army during FYs 2001–2011 (see Orvis et al., 2018). Table 2.1 reports first-term cumulative attrition rates.

Cost Estimates Used in Multiple Study Discussions

Appendix A discusses cost estimation for Basic Military Training, One Station Unit Training (OSUT), Advanced Individual Training (AIT), Initial Entry Training (IET), and overall recruiting costs. Appendix B covers training cost estimation for SF. These cost estimates are used in numerous studies discussed in Chapters 3 and 4 of this report. Additional cost estimates are used in discussions of multiple studies, although on a much more limited basis (e.g., two or three studies). We provide an overview of those types of additional cost estimates and their application in the following subsections. Cost estimates unique to specific studies or models are discussed in the respective write-ups.

Selective Reenlistment Bonuses Used in Retention Analyses

For our retention analyses, we calculated the SRB that would be needed to achieve the same increase in retention as the given study intervention (to a 50 percent retention rate). We interpolated between the values of adjacent percent increases in retention shown in Table 2.2. The required SRB size to achieve the same retention effect is the corresponding interpolated value for bonuses.

Recruiter Cost

Two of the studies discussed found a survey screening measure or demographic characteristics to be associated with recruiter productivity. We estimated the increase in recruiter productivity that could be achieved by using this information to screen out lower-preforming types of recruiters and replacing them with the types predicted to perform better. We used that calculation to estimate the number of recruiters that could be saved when holding required recruit production constant. Potential cost avoidance was estimated using the estimated savings in the number of recruiters needed given the improvement in productivity multiplied by $118,000 per recruiter (an Army-provided cost).[16]

Table 2.2. DRM-Based SRB

SRB Value	Increase in Retention (%)
5000	3.24
10,000	6.61
15,000	10.08
20,000	13.56
25,000	17.03
30,000	20.51
35,000	23.99
40,000	27.47
45,000	30.95

NOTE: Values provided by Michael Mattock and James Hosek using excursions of the DRM or derived from the information provided. Estimates are in 2015 dollars.

Cost to Convert Portions of Training Courses to Computer-Based Training

We estimated potential training cost avoided in the Army from reducing course length net of the cost of Computer-Based Training (CBT) conversion and maintenance. The calculations of net cost avoided required (1) choosing which Army courses to convert to CBT, (2) determination of the number of course hours reduced, (3) calculation of the cost of converting course hours to CBT, and (4) determination of the cost of training per course hour.

We chose courses similar to those reported in the underlying studies with sufficient throughput to justify conversion and the related weeks of training involved, at 40 training hours per week, to estimate total training hours. To be conservative, we assumed that the proportion of a course that could be converted and the reduction in length for those courses were consistent with the low end of the reported reductions in the studies. We then determined the number of enrollees per course hour saved, using a weighted average of course enrollments and lengths when multiple courses were involved.

The cost per hour to convert to CBT was estimated at $28,588 (Shanley et al., 2012, updated for inflation). It was assumed that conversion would be needed every six years and that maintenance costs per year were 25 percent of the conversion cost (Granja-Alvarez and

---

[16] See Study 6.1: Evaluation and Refinement of a Screening Instrument for U.S. Army Recruiters: Noncommissioned Officer Leadership Skills Inventory (Horgen et al., 2006).

Barranco-García, 1997). Thus, annualized cost per course hour to convert to CBT was calculated as $11,912 ($28,588, plus 0.25 of $28,588 multiplied by 6, all divided by 6).

Cost per training hour was derived from U.S. Army Training and Doctrine Command's (TRADOC's) Army Training Resource Model (ATRM) 159 (ATRM-159) analysis. We adjusted the cost per enrollee based on the course attrition rate (ATRRS, 2014) and inflated it to 2018 dollars. We then calculated the overall potential training cost avoided and subtracted the cost of course conversion and maintenance to estimate net potential cost avoidance.[17]

Cost of Injuries

In several studies, a regression analysis or raw data was used to compare injury rates between training program participants and control group members. We calculated the rates reported for men and for women and combined them into a single rate using the gender distribution of the FY 2017 accession cohort reported by the Center for Naval Analyses (83.25 percent men and 16.75 percent women among Army accessions).[18] We then applied the reported risk ratio or change in outcomes to the injury incidence rate to calculate a modified injury rate. We then multiplied the difference in injury rates by the size of the accession cohort to estimate the number of injuries saved. We multiplied the potential injuries avoided by the cost of an injury, estimated as we will describe.

Altarum Institute (2006) estimated that a musculoskeletal injury costs $3,020, which includes medical costs ($674), limited duty or lost days ($1,972), and medical hold ($374). We inflated medical costs and medical hold to 2018 dollars ($839 and $465, respectively). We adjusted limited duty or lost days by growth in military pay between 2006 and 2018. Specifically, the 2006 military pay table reported $1,936 per month for an E-4 with more than four years of service. The 2018 military pay table reported $2,491 per month for an E-4 with more than four years of service, an increase of 28.65 percent between 2006 and 2018. Adjusting the $1,972 limited duty or lost day portion of the injury cost estimate by 28.65 percent results in a cost of $2,537.[19]

The Altarum Institute estimate included service members across the total force. When using this estimate to calculate the potential savings resulting from fewer injuries during initial training, we needed to scale to E-1 pay. To do so, we used the Regular Military Compensation (RMC) Calculator to estimate pay for four types of soldiers:

---

[17] See Study 6.2: Navy Self-Paced Computer-Based Courses: Practical Implications of Saving Time Under Instruction (UI) (Carey, Reese, and Shuford, 2010) and Study 6.3: Online Training: An Evaluation of the Effectiveness and Efficiency of Training Law Enforcement Personnel over the Internet (Schmeeckle, 2003).

[18] Office of the Under Secretary of Defense, Personnel and Readiness, 2018.

[19] See Study 7.1: Effect of Pre-Accession Physical Fitness on Training Injuries Among US Army Recruits (Bedno et al., 2013); Study 7.2: The Victory Fitness Program: Influence of the US Army's Emerging Physical Readiness Training Doctrine on Fitness and Injuries in Basic Combat Training (Knapik et al., 2001); and Study 7.4: Influence of an Injury Reduction Program on Injury and Fitness Outcomes Among Soldiers (Knapik, Bullock, et al., 2004).

- E-1, 0 years of service, family size = 1, zip code 80918 (an average cost area): $18,176 per year in basic pay
- E-4, 4 years of service, family size = 1, zip code 80918: $53,047 per year in RMC
- E-4, 4 years of service, family size = 2, zip code 80918: $56,190 per year in RMC
- E-5, 6 years of service, family size = 3, zip code 80918: $62,343 per year in RMC.

We first computed the average RMC for the two E-4 soldiers ($54,619), then averaged that with the E-5 soldier, resulting in an average enlisted soldier who earns $58,481 per year. We applied the ratio of E-1 pay to this average soldier pay ($18,176 / $58,481) to the pay growth-inflated cost of limited duty or lost days and added it to the medical cost and medical hold portions of the overall cost estimate, i.e., $839 + $465 + $2,537 × 18,176 / 58,481 = $2,093 per musculoskeletal injury, for an initial trainee.

Cost of Drill Sergeant Instruction

These programs also involve a block of instruction to drill sergeants. We estimated the cost of one day of classroom training to be $1,046 using FY 2017 ATRM-159 estimates of the costs associated with providing training. In determining the number of drill sergeants needing to be trained, based on ATRRS information, we assumed a drill sergeant–to–soldier ratio of 1:20 but assumed that a drill sergeant can train four Basic Combat Training (BCT) sessions annually after being trained, yielding a ratio of 1:80 for a full accession cohort.[20]

Results Presented in This Report

We use a common format for reporting the results of our analysis. We begin by stating the study's objective and context, describe the results reported in the study, and then explain our analysis of the study's benefits and present our results in both text and a summary table.[21] There are several things to keep in mind when reading the descriptions of our analyses and reviewing the findings.

First, we make use of the most-detailed numbers available in the study and in our own data runs (e.g., our calculation of attrition rates) but round the numbers in our presentation. Therefore, multiplying the numbers in the summary table produces a result that is close to our final estimate of potential costs avoided but will not match exactly because of rounding.

---

[20] See Study 3.19: Evaluation of Two Army Fitness Programs: The TRADOC Standardized Physical Training Program for Basic Combat Training and the Fitness Assessment Program [Discharges Among Standardized Group Participants] (Knapik, Darakjy, et al., 2004); Study 7.2: The Victory Fitness Program: Influence of the US Army's Emerging Physical Readiness Training Doctrine on Fitness and Injuries in Basic Combat Training (Knapik et al., 2001); Study 7.3: Evaluation of Two Army Fitness Programs: The TRADOC Standardized Physical Training Program for Basic Combat Training and the Fitness Assessment Program [Injuries Among Standardized Group Participants] (Knapik, Darakjy, et al., 2004); and Study 7.4: Influence of an Injury Reduction Program on Injury and Fitness Outcomes Among Soldiers (Knapik, Bullock, et al., 2004).

[21] Listed below the results table is the full citation for the referenced study. Generally speaking, the studies describe results based on data collected during the period shortly preceding the research, unless otherwise noted.

Second, our practice of rounding in the presentation of results applies to the number of people in a calculation (e.g., number of potential accessions saved); we report fractions of people only when an intervention saved fewer than 25.

Third, we estimated confidence intervals for the primary outcome reported in the studies, such as the change in the attrition or retention rate. We then applied the lower and upper bound values of the effect size to reestimate the number of personnel affected (e.g., saved or retained) and carried that through the methodology described in each study to determine the estimated costs avoided. We considered increased reduction of certain serious legal incidents and fewer suicides as values in their own right and, therefore, did not do a cost analysis for these outcomes. We also found evidence of the success of certain interventions in reducing other legal incidents or adverse medical outcomes. However, we were unable to identify available cost measures associated with these outcomes. Consequently, additional research in these areas could be useful in quantifying their implications for potential cost avoidance relating to legal and medical interventions and their outcomes.

Caveats

Recruiting Cost When Screening Is Increased

In principle, decreasing potential enlisted supply (e.g., reducing the percentage of recruits allowed to come in with waivers, reducing the percentage of recruits with Tier 2 education credentials) should increase recruiting costs. However, the Recruiting Resource Model (RRM) (Knapp et al., 2018)–Recruit Selection Tool (Orvis et al., 2018) joint analysis shows that, for a 70,000-accession mission and a 6-percent unemployment rate (what the authors call "average conditions"), the effect on total cost is limited. For this reason, we do not reduce potential cost-avoidance estimates when screening out potential applicants.[22]

Unreported Research

Studies that find small or statistically insignificant effects may not be published, and it is not possible to systematically identify most of these studies. While we cannot directly control for studies not reported because of such findings, the *p*-values reported in the research studies described in this report provide relevant information concerning the likelihood that the result was a false positive. Note that the bias that is due to reporting only statistically significant results goes down as the sample size or effect size increases. For example, for studies using $p < 0.05$ for significance, we would expect 19 of every 20 studies reported to reflect actual significance. At $p < 0.01$, it would be 99 of every 100 studies. At $p < 0.001$, it would be 999 of every 1,000 studies, and so forth. In addition, more replications of the results increase confidence that the

[22] See Study 6.4: Resources Required to Meet Army's Enlisted Recruiting Requirements Under Alternative Recruiting Goals, Conditions, and Eligibility Policies (Knapp et al., 2018).

finding was not simply a false positive. Much of the material in our chapters reports findings for the same or similar predictors, and the typical *p*-value is $p < 0.01$ or lower.

Overall Costs for Intervention Programs

The cost of programs having substantial execution costs is accounted for in the individual study discussions. We discussed relevant costs for the elements of some of the programs in the previous section. Additional details on the application of these cost elements and other program cost estimations are provided throughout the report in the study write-ups. When such program costs are involved, they are netted out of the outcome-based estimated savings as part of the estimation of potential cost avoided. When the estimated annual program cost exceeds the estimated annual savings from the outcome, the implication is that money could be saved by terminating the program.

Incremental Costs of Psychological Screening Measures

Numerous studies detailed in this report found that the application of psychological screening measures could reduce adverse outcomes and, in our analyses, related costs. These analyses do not consider the cost of administering and evaluating the psychological screening measures. The costs are likely dwarfed by the potential cost avoidance resulting from improved outcomes.

Cost of Conducting a Study

We do not discuss the cost of conducting the individual research studies covered in this report. These one-time costs would be minimal compared with the potential cost avoidance resulting from the improved outcomes reported in nearly all the studies discussed.

Use of the Reported Results

Each of the write-ups in this report examines potential outcomes for the screener(s), intervention(s), or other factor(s) reported in that particular study. We have not attempted to analyze the benefits of combining factors across studies. Similarly, we have not attempted to assess the incremental benefit of applying the factor(s) discussed in a study in the current environment. Therefore, our analyses should be viewed as an approach for translating changes in outcomes in social science research into the value of those changes, not as recommendations to implement the screener(s), intervention(s), or other factor(s) that induced changes in outcomes.

Chapter 3. Initial Training Attrition

This chapter presents information on the potential annual costs avoided from lowering training attrition through the use of personality tests or other screeners. Table 3.1 categorizes the studies considered in this chapter, providing full titles and assigning study numbers.

Unless otherwise indicated, all effect sizes are in percentage points.

Table 3.1. Initial Training Attrition

Study Number	Name of Study
Studies Involving Psychological Screeners That Could Reduce Initial Training Attrition Among All Recruits	
3.1	Assessing the Tailored Adaptive Personality Assessment System (TAPAS) as an MOS Qualification Instrument (Nye et al., 2012)
3.2	Expanded Enlistment Eligibility Metrics (EEEM): Recommendations on a Non-Cognitive Screen for New Soldier Selection (AIM, TAPAS, RBI) (Knapp and Heffner, 2010)
3.3	Predicting Discharge from Air Force Basic Training by Pattern of Affect (Lubin, Fielder, and Whitlock, 1999)
Studies Involving Psychological Screeners That Could Reduce Initial Training Attrition Among Certain MOSs	
3.4	The "Big Five" Personality Factors in the IPI and MMPI: Predictors of Police Performance (Cortina et al., 1992)
3.5	Psychological Measures as Predictors of Military Training Performance (Hartmann et al., 2003) and Rorschach Variables and Big Five Scales as Predictors of Military Training Completion: A Replication Study of the Selection of Candidates to the Naval Special Forces in Norway (Hartmann and Grønnerød, 2009)
3.6	Psychological Hardiness Predicts Success in US Army Special Forces Candidates (Bartone et al., 2008)
3.7	Assessing the Tailored Adaptive Personality Assessment System (Nye et al., 2014)
3.8	Predictive Validity of an Automated Personality Inventory for Air Force Pilot Selection (Siem, 1990)
3.9	The Unique Contribution of Selected Personality Tests to the Prediction of Success in Naval Pilot Training (Street, Helton, and Dolgin, 1992)
3.10	Predicting Training Success with the NEO-PI-R: The Use of Logistic Regression to Determine the Odds of Completing a Pilot Screening Program (Anesgart and Callister, 2001)
Studies Involving Nonpsychological (Other) Screeners That Could Reduce Initial-Training Attrition Among All Recruits	
3.11	Expanded Enlistment Eligibility Metrics (EEEM): Recommendations on a Non-Cognitive Screen for New Soldier Selection (Assembling Objects, WPA Dimensions, WPA Facets) (Knapp and Heffner, 2010)
3.12	Attrition in the Army from the Signing of the Enlistment Contract Through 180 Days of Service (Fischl and Blackwell, 2000)
Studies Involving Nonpsychological (Other) Screeners That Could Reduce Initial-Training Attrition Among Certain MOSs	
3.13	*The Roles of Perseverance, Cognitive Ability, and Physical Fitness in U.S. Army Special Forces Assessment and Selection* (Beal, 2010)

Study Number	Name of Study
3.14	Air Force Officer Qualifying Test (AFOQT): Predictors of Undergraduate Pilot Training and Undergraduate Navigator Training Success (Arth et al., 1990)
3.15	Air Force Officer Training School Selection System Validation (Cowan, Barrett, and Wegner, 1990)
Studies Involving Physical Training Interventions That Could Reduce Initial Training Attrition Among All Recruits	
3.16	Outcomes of Fort Jackson's Physical Training and Rehabilitation Program in Army Basic Combat Training: Return to Training, Graduation, and 2-Year Retention (Hauret et al., 2004)
3.17	Retention in Service of Recruits Assigned to the Army Physical Fitness Test Enhancement Program in Basic Combat Training (Knapik et al., 2003)
3.18	Evaluation of Two Army Fitness Programs: The TRADOC Standardized Physical Training Program for Basic Combat Training and the Fitness Assessment Program (Discharges Among Standardized Group Participants) (Knapik, Darakjy, et al., 2004)
3.19	Evaluation of Two Army Fitness Programs: The TRADOC Standardized Physical Training Program for Basic Combat Training and the Fitness Assessment Program (Discharges Among Fitness Assessment Program Participants) (Knapik, Darakjy, et al., 2004)

NOTE: AIM = Assessment of Individual Motivation; IPI = Inwald Personality Inventory; MMPI = Minnesota Multiphasic Personality Inventory; MOS = Military Occupational Specialty; NEO-PI-R = NEO Personality Inventory–Revised; RBI = Rational Biodata Inventory; WPA = Work Preferences Assessment.

Studies Involving Psychological Screeners That Could Reduce Initial Training Attrition Among All Recruits

3.1: Assessing the Tailored Adaptive Personality Assessment System (TAPAS) as an MOS Qualification Instrument (Nye et al., 2012)

Description of the Study

This study examines whether TAPAS may be useful for selecting and classifying recruits. The key issues were to identify whether using TAPAS scales could improve MOS screening and to provide improved estimates of performance potential, including reducing attrition. Using predicted performance scores for each individual, the research studied whether placement into an MOS on the basis of TAPAS scores could increase performance, improve attitudes, and reduce attrition. The study reported the association of TAPAS composites with six-month attrition rates within four MOSs, reported as a multiple regression statistic: 11B (infantry), 0.22; 31B (military police), 0.27; 68W (combat medic), 0.18; and 88M (motor transport operator), 0.18.

RAND Arroyo Center Analysis

We used the multiple R measures of the effectiveness of the TAPAS composites in predicting attrition within each MOS. These were combined into one measure with a sample weighted average (0.21), weighted by the relative size of each MOS (8,739; 2,307; 3,292; and 2,872, for 11B, 31B, 68W, and 88M, respectively). Because the effect size is calculated from a range of MOSs (one each from the combat, combat support, combat service support, and special branches), the potential savings in recruiting and training costs were calculated using the entire accession population.

As described in Chapter 2, the effect size is the multiple R (0.21) times the standard deviation of the six-month attrition rate (see Table 2.1, 32.01 percent). The 918 potential annual accessions saved statistic is calculated by multiplying the effect size (6.72 percentage points) by Z_x (0.195, the mean standard normal distribution z-score after removing the lowest 10 percent of z-scores) by annual accessions (70,000). The costs of first-term attrition were estimated to be $75,638 per each accession to produce an IET graduate, based on the cost of successfully recruiting a single accession plus the sample-weighted costs of a graduate of BCT/AIT or OSUT, as described in Appendix A. Using this information, we then calculated the potential annual costs avoided as $69.4 million (918 times $75,638). Table 3.2 summarizes the key information.

Table 3.2. Potential Annual Costs Avoided as a Result of Using the TAPAS as an MOS Qualification Instrument

Screener	Effect Size (*RxSDy*) (%)	Z_x	Annual Accessions	Potential Annual Accessions Saved	Recruiting and Training Costs ($)	Potential Annual Costs Avoided ($M)
TAPAS	6.72 [4.96, 8.48]	0.195	70,000	918 [678, 1,158]	75,638	69.4 [51.2, 87.6]

SOURCES: Study documented in Christopher D. Nye, Fritz Drasgow, Oleksandr S. Chernyshenko, Stephen Stark, U. Christean Kubisiak, Leonard A. White, and Irwin Jose, *Assessing the Tailored Adaptive Personality Assessment System (TAPAS) as an MOS Qualification Instrument*, Personnel Decisions Research Institute (PDRI) Inc., 2012. Recruiting and training costs derived from HQDA G-1 and ATRRS, FY 2018.

3.2: Expanded Enlistment Eligibility Metrics (EEEM): Recommendations on a Non-Cognitive Screen for New Soldier Selection (AIM, TAPAS, RBI) (Knapp and Heffner, 2010)

Description of the Study

The purpose of this study was to provide recommendations to the Army on experimental noncognitive predictor measures that could enhance entry-level soldier selection and classification decisions. The AFQT is a useful screener for selecting new soldiers; this study was designed to identify additional metrics, particularly those that identify noncognitive attributes, such as temperament, interests, and values, that could potentially be used to augment the AFQT. The EEEM project focuses on initial soldier selection. This EEEM study uses a subset of the Army Class data.

The report displays the incremental validity of several screeners in predicting six-month attrition over an AFQT-only model. Each screener-AFQT combination was compared with AFQT-only results. Six different screeners (AIM, TAPAS, RBI, Assembling Objects, WPA

Dimensions, and WPA Facets) showed statistically significant improvements over AFQT alone. In this write-up, we present the results for AIM, TAPAS, and RBI.[1]

RAND Arroyo Center Analysis

The cost avoidance was based the percentage reduction of attrition from the potential inclusion of these screeners in the selection and classification process. The effect sizes were the incremental validity of each screener (reported as the change in Nagelkerke's R over the AFQT-only model (0.162 for AIM, 0.195 for TAPAS, and 0.193 for RBI), times the standard deviation of six-month attrition. These effect sizes were placed into our framework, cutting off the bottom 10 percent of the screener score distribution. The potential annual-accessions-saved statistics were calculated by multiplying the effect sizes by Z_x by annual accessions. Given the cost of an IET graduate, we then calculated potential annual costs avoided for each screener. Table 3.3 summarizes the key information.

Table 3.3. Potential Annual Costs Avoided from Using a Noncognitive Screen for New-Soldier Selection

Screener	Effect Size ($RxSD_y$)	Z_x	Annual Accessions	Potential Annual Accessions Saved	Recruiting and Training Costs	Potential Annual Costs Avoided
AIM	5.19% [3.66%, 6.72%]	0.195	70,000	708 [499, 917]	$75,638	$53.5M [$37.7M, $69.4M]
TAPAS	6.24% [4.74%, 7.74%]	0.195	70,000	852 [647, 1,057]	$75,638	$64.4M [$49.0M, $79.9M]
RBI	6.18% [4.94%,7.42%]	0.195	70,000	843 [674, 1,012]	$75,638	$63.8M [$51.0M, $76.6M]

SOURCES: Study documented in Deidre J.Knapp and Tonia S. Heffner, *Expanded Enlistment Eligibility Metrics (EEEM): Recommendations on a Non-Cognitive Screen for New Soldier Selection*, U.S. Army Research Institute for the Behavioral and Social Sciences, 2010. Recruiting and training costs derived from ATRRS and HQDA G-1, FY 2018.

3.3: Predicting Discharge from Air Force Basic Training by Pattern of Affect (Lubin, Fielder, and Whitlock, 1999)

Description of the Study

This study examines how effective the state form of the Multiple Affect Adjective Check List–Revised (MAACL-R), a list of 132 adjectives with affective connotations, is in predicting success in Air Force Basic Training. The study examined 200 Air Force recruits who completed the MAACL-R by indicating the extent to which each of the adjectives applied to them at the time they completed the questionnaire. The authors used five factorially derived scales (anxiety,

[1] Assembling Objects, WPA Dimensions, and WPA Facets are covered later, in the discussion of Study 3.11: Expanded Enlistment Eligibility Metrics (EEEM): Recommendations on a Non-Cognitive Screen for New Soldier Selection (Assembling Objects, WPA Dimensions, WPA Facets).

depression, hostility, positive affect, and sensation-seeking) and two composite scales (dysphoria, the combination of anxiety, depression, and hostility, and PASS, the combination of positive affect and sensation-seeking) to evaluate the relationship between scores on the MAACL-R and completion of basic training.

Among study participants, 157 graduated from basic training, and 26 were discharged, a pass rate of 86 percent (17 recruits were dropped from the analysis, three had missing data, and 14 were considered outliers). The canonical correlation between completion of basic training and the unipolar scales (anxiety, depression, hostility, positive affect, and sensation seeking) was 0.42, and the correlation with composite scales (dysphoria and PASS) was 0.36, both of which were statistically significant.

RAND Arroyo Center Analysis

The effect size is the product of the correlation between a MAACL-R scale score and basic training completion times the standard deviation of the basic training completion rate (14.7 percent for the unipolar scales and 12.6 percent for the composite scales). We then removed the bottom 10 percent of scorers on the MAACL-R and multiplied by 70,000 annual accessions to estimate potential accessions saved. Finally, we multiplied by the cost of basic training to estimate potential annual costs avoided, as shown in Appendix A. Table 3.4 summarizes the results.

Table 3.4. Potential Annual Costs Avoided from Using the MAACL-R to Predict Success in Basic Training

Screener	Effect Size ($RxSD_y$)	Z_x	Annual Accessions	Potential Accessions Saved	Recruiting and Training Costs	Potential Annual Costs Avoided
MAACL-R unipolar scales	14.7% [10.07%, 19.33%]	0.195	70,000	2,002 [1,372, 2,632]	$47,430	$94.9M [$65.0M, $124.8M]
MAACL-R composite scales	12.6% [7.84%, 17.36%]	0.195	70,000	1,716 [1,068, 2,364]	$47,430	$81.4M [$50.6M, $112.1M]

SOURCES: Study documented in Bernard Lubin, Edna R. Fielder, and Rodney Van Whitlock, "Predicting Discharge from Air Force Basic Training by Pattern of Affect," Journal of Clinical Psychology, Vol. 55, No. 1, January 1999. Additional information from HQDA G-1 and TRADOC (ATRRS) information, FY 2018.

Studies Involving Psychological Screeners That Could Reduce Initial Training Attrition Among Certain MOSs

3.4: The "Big Five" Personality Factors in the IPI and MMPI: Predictors of Police Performance (Cortina et al., 1992)

Description of the Study

The study evaluated the validity of Big Five (openness to experience, conscientiousness, extraversion, agreeableness, neuroticism) personality factors in predicting dropouts in police training in Michigan. Two personality inventories were used: the IPI and the MMPI. The IPI was designed specifically for use in public safety and security assessment, and research has shown that police officer candidates exhibit identifiable profiles on the MMPI.

The study reported that 27 percent of police candidates dropped out of the six-month police training course. Among the ten personality-based predictors of the IPI and MMPI, six were statistically significantly correlated with turnover: MMPI Neuroticism ($r = 0.27$), MMPI Extraversion ($r = 0.21$), MMPI Conscientious ($r = 0.17$), IPI Neuroticism ($r = 0.19$), IPI Extraversion ($r = 0.19$), and IPI Agreeableness ($r = 0.17$).

RAND Arroyo Center Analysis

To calculate potential costs avoided from reducing turnover in police training, we multiplied these correlations by the standard deviation of turnover to get the effect size, where the turnover rate reported in the study was 27 percent. Then, to put these results into an Army context, we removed the bottom 10 percent of scorers on each of the statistically significant predictors and multiplied the number of trainees saved by the cost of an MP OSUT graduate.

The replacement cost for a MP course graduate was derived from information from HQDA G-1, plus ATRRS information for MP OSUT in 2017. According to the G-1 information, the average cost of an OSUT graduate was $30,350 (including the cost of $650 for the reception battalion) for a 14.8-week course (from ATRRS). Because MP OSUT was a 19.2-week course, we proportionally increased the estimated cost to $39,373 for that course. We then added the cost of accession (including the cost of processing through U.S. Military Entrance Processing Command [USMEPCOM]) for a MP graduate, taking into account the 17.6 percent MP OSUT attrition rate (ATRRS, 2018), which implies that it takes 1.214 accessions [1 / (1 – 0.176)] to get a MP graduate. Thus, the accession related cost of a MP graduate was $32,933 (1.214 times $27,137, the cost of an accession). Adding the MP OSUT cost and the accession-related cost yielded a replacement cost for MP OSUT of $72,306 ($39,373 plus $32,933). Appendix A presents the recruiting and training costs (e.g., cost of an OSUT graduate, cost of accession) used to derive MP OSUT costs.

For each predictor, the potential annual accessions saved statistics are calculated by multiplying the effect sizes by Z_x by annual MP accessions (4,104). Given the cost of an MP

OSUT graduate, we then calculated potential annual costs avoided for each screener. Table 3.5 summarizes the key information.

Table 3.5. Potential Annual Costs Avoided from Using Big Five Personality Factors to Predict Police Performance

Screener	Effect Size ($rxSD_y$)	Z_x	Annual MP Accessions	Potential Annual Accessions Saved	MP Recruiting and Training Costs	Potential Annual Costs Avoided
MMPI Neuroticism	12% [7.25%, 16.75%]	0.195	4,104	96 [58, 134]	$72,306	$6.9M [$4.2M, $9.7M]
MMPI Extraversion	9.3% [4.50%, 14.10%]	0.195	4,104	75 [36, 114]	$72,306	$5.4M [$2.6M, $8.2M]
MMPI Conscientious	7.6% [2.71%, 12.49%]	0.195	4,104	60 [21, 99]	$72,306	$4.4M [$1.6M, $7.2M]
IPI Neuroticism	8.4% [3.58%, 13.22%]	0.195	4,104	68 [29, 107]	$72,306	$4.9M [$2.1M, $7.7M]
IPI Extraversion	8.4% [3.58%, 13.22%]	0.195	4,104	68 [29, 107]	$72,306	$4.9M [$2.1M, $7.7M]
IPI Agreeableness	7.6% [2.71%, 12.49%]	0.195	4,104	60 [21, 99]	$72,306	$4.4M [$1.6M, $7.2M]

SOURCES: Study documented in Cortina, Jose M., Mary L. Doherty, Neal Schmitt, Gary Kaufman, and Richard G. Smith, "The 'Big Five' Personality Factors in the IPI and MMPI: Predictors of Police Performance," Personnel Psychology, Vol. 45, No. 1, 1992. Additional information from MP OSUT throughput from ATRRS.

3.5: Psychological Measures as Predictors of Military Training Performance (Hartmann et al., 2003) and Rorschach Variables and Big Five Scales as Predictors of Military Training Completion: A Replication Study of the Selection of Candidates to the Naval Special Forces in Norway (Hartmann and Grønnerød, 2009)

Description of the Study

This research evaluated the predictive validity of various psychological measures in determining who would pass the Naval Special Forces (NSF) training in Norway. NSF training is a four-week program involving intense and highly demanding physical and psychological challenges, somewhat similar to the Special Forces Assessment and Selection (SFAS) course in the Army. In Hartmann et al., 2003, only 38 percent (27 of 71) of the NSF candidates in the authors' sample successfully completed the training. In Hartmann and Grønnerød, 2009, only 22 percent (31 of 140) successfully completed the training. Various screeners were administered to male applicants at NSF, including the Rorschach personality test. Rorschach variables were significantly correlated with passing the NSF training, supporting the idea that they could be used to predict NSF training performance.

RAND Arroyo Center Analysis

We estimated the extent to which SF recruiting and training costs (through the SFAS course) could be avoided by applying the most effective Rorschach scale in Hartmann et al., 2003, and Hartmann and Grønnerød, 2009, to the Army context. In particular, we applied our standard method for correlations to the correlations reported for training completion in Table 4 and Table 3 of the respective studies and the related pass rates reported.

We found that the variable "x-%" ($r = -0.48$) and the variable "m," ($r = -0.25$) in the first and second studies, respectively, had the largest effect on the pass rate. In the first study, the product of the correlation with the standard error of the pass rate (effect size) was –23.30 percent; after the bottom 10 percent of scorers on that variable was eliminated, the estimated change in pass rate was 4.54 percentage points. In the second study, by analogy, the estimated effect size was –10.38 percent, and the change in the estimated pass rate after removing the bottom 10 percent was 2.02 percentage points. Multiplying these estimated improvements in the pass rate by 2,701 trainees provided the estimated trainees saved. We multiplied estimated trainees saved by the cost of an SFAS graduate to calculate potential costs avoided. Table 3.6 summarizes the key information.

Table 3.6. Potential Annual Costs Avoided from Using the Psychological Measures as Predictors of Special Forces Training Performance

Screener	Effect Size (*rxSDy*)	*Zx*	FY 2013 SFAS starts	Potential SFAS Trainees Saved	Recruiting and Training Costs Through SFAS	Potential Annual Costs Avoided
Rorschach Scale	–23.3% [–13.25%, –33.35%]	–0.195	2,701	123 [70, 176]	$72,033	$8.8M [$5.0M, $12.7M]
Rorschach Scale	–10.38% [–3.67%, –17.09%]	–0.195	2,701	55 [19, 91]	$72,033	$3.9M [$1.4M, $6.6M]

SOURCES: Study documented in Ellen Hartmann and Cato Grønnerød, "Rorschach Variables and Big Five Scales as Predictors of Military Training Completion: A Replication Study of the Selection of Candidates to the Naval Special Forces in Norway," Journal of Personality Assessment, Vol. 91, No. 3, May 2009, and Ellen Hartmann, Tor Sunde, Wenche Kristensen, and Monica Martinussen, "Psychological Measures as Predictors of Military Training Performance," Journal of Personality Assessment, Vol. 80, No. 1, March 2003. Additional information from briefing slide received from U.S. Army John F. Kennedy Special Warfare Center and School (SWCS) on SFAS starts. Recruitment and training costs per graduate are derived in separate tables. Primary sources are Military Personnel, Accessions (MPA) within HQDA G-1; TRADOC and ATRM-159 course reports; and the Special Operations Recruiting Battalion (SORB). Also see Appendix B.

3.6: Psychological Hardiness Predicts Success in US Army Special Forces Candidates (Bartone et al., 2008)

Description of the Study

This research examined the selection of soldiers for enrollment in the SFAS course, the first step in qualifying for SF. A substantial percentage of SFAS candidates normally fail to successfully complete the training. The authors looked to improve the selection of candidates for

SFAS by applying a screener at the beginning of SFAS that assessed the psychological hardiness of the applicants. Scores from the short form of the Dispositional Resilience Scale were obtained from 1,138 SFAS candidates in the mid-2000s, then used as an independent variable in a logistic regression for predicting successful completion of the course.

The findings showed that 56 percent (637) of the authors' 1,138 sample of candidates graduated from SFAS. The analysis also confirmed that SFAS graduates were significantly higher in psychological hardiness than were nongraduates (mean score 34.34 versus 33.73). Using a logistic regression approach, the authors estimated an odds ratio for a one-point increase in the hardiness score of 1.033 (page 79 of study).

RAND Arroyo Center Analysis

To estimate potential costs avoided, we reduced SF recruiting and training costs (through the SFAS course) by applying the authors' study of the SFAS course to the current Army situation and screening on hardiness scores. The mean hardiness score in the authors' sample was 34.07 (Table 1 of study). Assuming that hardiness scores were normally distributed, we computed a revised mean after dropping scores in the bottom 10 percent the distribution. The new mean was computed as the old mean plus Z_x times the standard deviation of the hardiness scores, which was 4.3 percentage points (Table 1). Thus, the new mean was 34.91 (34.07 plus 0.195 times 4.3), an increase of 0.84. Using the odds ratio from the logistic regression results, the decrease in attrition from using hardiness scores as a screener was 0.67 percent.[2] Based on 2,701 annual SFAS starts (SWCS-provided information), we estimated the number of SFAS trainees saved as a result of the reduction in attrition (18) and multiply by the cost of an SFAS graduate (see Appendix B) to estimate potential annual costs avoided, as shown in Table 3.7.

Table 3.7. Potential Annual Costs Avoided from Using Psychological Hardiness to Predict Success in SFAS

Screener	Decrease in Attrition	Annual SFAS Starts	Potential Annual SFAS Trainees Saved	Recruiting and Training Costs Through SFAS	Potential Annual Costs Avoided
Psychological hardiness	0.67% [0.42%, 0.92%]	2,701	18 [11, 25]	$72.033	$1.3M [$0.8M, $1.8M]

SOURCES: Study documented in Paul T. Bartone, Robert R. Roland, James J. Picano, and Thomas J. Williams, "Psychological Hardiness Predicts Success in US Army Special Forces Candidates," International Journal of Selection and Assessment, Vol. 16, No. 1, 2008. SFAS starts from SWCS-provided information. Recruitment and training costs per graduate are derived in separate table. Primary sources are MPA, TRADOC, and ATRM-159 course reports, and the SORB.

---

[2] This is calculated by adjusting the odds ratio to 1.028 for a 0.84- versus 1-point increase in the hardiness score [$0.033 \times 0.84 + 1$]. This means that $(p2/q2) / (p1/q1) = 1.028$, where $p2$ is the new SFAS success rate and $p1$ is the original pass rate (637/1138), and $q = 1 - p$. Solving for $p2$ yields a new pass rate of 56.65 percent, an increase of 0.67 percentage points.

3.7: Assessing the Tailored Adaptive Personality Assessment System (Nye et al., 2014)

Description of the Study

This research examined whether the TAPAS may be useful as a screener for identifying soldiers who will perform well in an Army SFAS course. Between February and June 2012, TAPAS data were collected from 1,216 soldier candidates attending SFAS just before the course began. The study developed scales and an empirical model from the TAPAS results in an effort to improve the selection of SFAS trainees.

The results of the study indicated that several scales were significantly related to soldier selection. Using a composite scale as a predictor, the authors found that only 35 percent of soldiers in the lowest quintile in the scale were selected to continue after SFAS, while 61 percent in the highest quintile were selected. Thus, the authors concluded the TAPAS was useful for differentiating candidates who were successfully selected for further Army Special Operations Forces training from soldiers who were voluntarily or involuntarily dropped from the course.

RAND Arroyo Center Analysis

We estimated the extent to which SF recruiting and training costs up through SFAS could be avoided by screening out the bottom 10 percent of applicants using TAPAS. We applied data reported on quintiles of the likelihood of qualification in Nye et al., 2014, approximating the effect of taking 10 percent from the bottom quintile and proportionally distributing the scores of replacement candidates over the remaining quintiles (each of which will contain 22.5 percent of the new sample). We calculated the new qualification rate from the adjusted data on quintiles (49.85 percent versus 48.20 percent), then the change in selection rates (effect size, 1.65 percentage points). We then calculated the number of SFAS trainees saved and the related estimated potential cost avoidance. Table 3.8 presents the details of our analysis.

Table 3.8. Potential Annual Costs Avoided from Using TAPAS to Predict Success in SFAS

Screener	Decrease in Attrition	FY 2013 SFAS Starts	Potential Annual SFAS Trainees Saved	Recruiting and Training Costs Through SFAS	Potential Annual Costs Avoided
TAPAS	1.65%	2,701	45	$72,033	$3.2M
	[1.27%, 2.03%]		[35, 55]		[$2.5M, $4.0M]

SOURCES: Study documented in Christopher D. Nye, Scott A. Beal, Fritz Drasgow, J. Douglas Dressel, Leonard A. White, and Stephen Stark, *Assessing the Tailored Adaptive Personality Assessment System, U.S. Army Research Institute for the Behavioral and Social Sciences*, 2014. SFAS starts from SWCS-provided information. Training costs per graduate for SFAS are derived in a separate table in Appendix B. Primary sources are MPA, TRADOC, and ATRM-159 course reports, and the SORB.

3.8: Predictive Validity of an Automated Personality Inventory for Air Force Pilot Selection (Siem, 1990)

Description of the Study

The study evaluated whether a personality inventory, the Automated Aircrew Personality Profiler, was effective in predicting success in pilot training. The profiler combined 16 subtests, from which five personality scores were computed: hostility, self-confidence, values flexibility, depression, and mania.

The pass rate from pilot training was 82 percent among study participants. Three of the personality factor scores correlated statistically significantly with passing Undergraduate Pilot Training (UPT): hostility ($r = -0.12$), self-confidence ($r = 0.13$), and values flexibility ($r = 0.12$).

RAND Arroyo Center Analysis

The effect size is the correlation between a personality factor scale and graduation from UPT times the standard deviation of the UPT pass rate (–4.61 percent for hostility, 4.99 percent for self-confidence, and 4.61 percent for values flexibility). We then removed the bottom 10 percent of scorers for each of the personality factors.

We used the Department of the Army (DA) FY 2019 budget estimates to determine the total number of fixed-wing pilot trainees in the Army. The FY 2019 budget estimates report the number of trainees in each year, FYs 2017–2019, which we used to compute an average (108 trainees per year) (DA, 2018). We multiplied the effect size by 0.195 (removing the bottom 10 percent of scorers) by 108 trainees, which results in the potential trainees saved. We multiplied the number of potential trainees saved by the cost of fixed-wing pilot training (based on ATRM-159) to estimate potential annual costs avoided. Table 3.9 shows the results.

Table 3.9. Potential Annual Cost Avoided from Using the Automated Aircrew Personality Profile to Predict Success in Undergraduate Pilot Training

Screener	Effect Size ($rxSD_y$)	Z_x	Annual Trainees	Potential Trainees Saved	Training Cost	Potential Annual Cost Avoided
Hostility	–4.61% [–8.77%, –0.45%]	–0.195	108	0.97 [0.09, 1.85]	$221,698	$0.2M [$0.02M, $0.4M]
Self-confidence	4.99% [0.84%, 9.14%]	0.195	108	1.05 [0.18, 1.92]	$221,698	$0.2M [$0.04M, $0.4M]
Values Flexibility	4.61% [0.45%, 8.77%]	0.195	108	0.97 [0.09, 1.85]	$221,698	$0.2M [$0.02M, $0.4M]

SOURCES: Study documented in Frederick M. Siem, "Predictive Validity of an Automated Personality Inventory for Air Force Pilot Selection," *International Journal of Aviation Psychology*, Vol. 2, No. 4, 1990. The cost of fixed-wing pilot training ($221,698) was based on ATRM-159. The number of annual trainees was estimated using DA FY 2019 budget estimates, which reported trainees in each year, FYs 2017–2019. We used the average across all three years (DA, 2018).

3.9: *The Unique Contribution of Selected Personality Tests to the Prediction of Success in Naval Pilot Training* (Street, Helton, and Dolgin, 1992)

Description of the Study

This study examines whether the Aviation Qualification Test (AQT), Flight Aptitude Rating (FAR), and Pilot Personality Questionnaire (PPQ) are able to predict whether trainees pass naval flight training. The AQT/FAR is a series of multiple-choice tests. The AQT measures general intelligence, verbal and quantitative abilities, clerical skills, and situational judgement. The FAR is made up of a Mechanical Comprehension Test, the Spatial Apperception Test, and the Biographical Inventory. The PPQ is a set of four personality tests.

Among the study participants who completed the AFQ/FAR prior to selection for aviation training and the PPQ as part of a continuing selection research project, 168 passed naval flight training, and 43 failed, an overall pass rate of 79.6 percent. The Pearson correlation coefficient between AQT/FAR and PPQ and success in naval flight training is 0.28.

RAND Arroyo Center Analysis

We calculated the effect size using the correlation coefficient times the standard deviation of the pass rate. We then screened out the bottom 10 percent of scorers on the AQT/FAR and PPQ and multiplied by the number of annual fixed-wing pilot trainees, which produced the number of potential trainees saved by using the AQT/FAR and PPQ as screeners. We multiplied the number of potential trainees saved by the cost of training. Table 3.10 shows the results.

Table 3.10. Potential Annual Cost Avoided Due to Screening on the AQT/FAR and PPQ for Fixed-Wing Pilot Training

Screener	Effect Size ($rxSD_y$)	Z_x	Annual Trainees	Potential Trainees Saved	Training Cost	Potential Annual Cost Avoided
AQT/FAR and PPQ	11.3% [6.05%, 16.55%]	0.195	108	2.38 [1.27, 3.49]	$221,698	$0.5M [$0.3M, $0.8M]

SOURCES: Study documented in D. R. Street, Jr., K. T. Helton, and D. L. Dolgin, *The Unique Contribution of Selected Personality Tests to the Prediction of Success in Naval Pilot Training*, Naval Aerospace Medical Research Laboratory, 1992.

NOTES: We calculated the cost of fixed-wing pilot training ($221,698). Air Force fixed-wing pilot training consists of 40 days of Initial Flight Screening, followed by approximately one year of Specialized UPT (SUPT). The number of annual trainees was estimated using DA FY 2019 budget estimates, which reported trainees in each year, FY 2017–2019. We used the average across all three years (DA, 2018).

3.10: Predicting Training Success with the NEO-PI-R: The Use of Logistic Regression to Determine the Odds of Completing a Pilot Screening Program (Anesgart and Callister, 2001)

Description of the Study

This study used NEO PI-R, which measures the Big Five personality domains (neuroticism, extraversion, openness, agreeableness, and conscientiousness), to describe a technique to predict pilot training success. The study reports the number of trainees who completed the Enhanced Flight Screening Program and the number who left because of self-initiated termination for five levels of neuroticism: for very low neuroticism, one trainee left and 63 completed; for low, four trainees left and 217 completed; for average, five trainees left and 378 completed; for high, 16 trainees left and 195 completed; and for very high levels of neuroticism, five trainees left and 54 completed.

RAND Arroyo Center Analysis

Using the numbers just described, the original failure rate among study participants was 3.30 percent (1 + 4 + 5+ 16 + 5 = 31, out of a total of 938 trainees). We removed the bottom 10 percent (94 trainees) of neuroticism scorers, which includes all the trainees who scored very high on the neuroticism scale, and 35 who scored high. To determine how many of the remaining high scorers would have failed pilot training, we subtracted 35 from the original 211 trainees in that category and multiplied by the original failure rate in that category (16 / 211 = 7.58 percent). Therefore, among the remaining 176 (211 – 35) trainees with a high neuroticism score, 13 would fail training (176 × 0.0758). The new failure rate among trainees is 2.77 percent (1 + 4 + 5 + 13, out of 844 trainees), a reduction in the failure rate of 0.54 percentage points.

According to the DA FY 2019 budget estimate, there were 108 fixed-wing pilot trainees per year between FYs 2017 and 2019. Navigator trainees also participate in the Enhanced Flight Screening Program, the course that trainees were enrolling in when they took the NEO-PI-R. According to Cowan, Barrett, and Wegner, 1990, the Air Force trains a bit under four times as many pilots as navigators, so we used the same ratio and estimated that the Army trains approximately 25 navigators per year. Therefore, the sample size for analysis is 108 pilots plus 25 navigators, or 133 trainees.

Air Force fixed-wing pilot training consists of 40 days of initial Flight Screening, followed by approximately one year of SUPT. We prorated the full cost ($221,698) by 40 days to determine the cost of the Enhanced Flight Screening Program.

We multiplied the reduction in the failure rate by the number of pilot and navigator trainees to determine the number of potential trainees saved. We then multiplied the number of potential trainees saved by the cost of the Enhanced Flight Screening portion of pilot training to estimate the potential annual costs avoided. Table 3.11 shows the results.

Table 3.11. Potential Annual Cost Avoided from Using the NEO-PI-R to Screen Students in the Enhanced Flight Screening Program

Screener	Reduction in Attrition	Annual Trainees	Potential Trainees Saved	Training Cost	Potential Annual Cost Avoided
NEO-PI-R	0.54% [0.22%, 0.86%]	133	0.72 [0.29, 1.15]	$22,170	$0.02M [$0.006M, $0.03M]

SOURCES: Study documented in Martin N. Anesgart and Joseph D. Callister, *Predicting Training Success with the NEO-PI-R: The Use of Logistic Regression to Determine the Odds of Completing a Pilot Screening Program*, Air Force Research Laboratory, Human Effectiveness Directorate, 2001.
NOTE: The number of annual trainees was estimated using DA FY 2019 budget estimates, which reported trainees in each year, FYs 2017–2019. We used the average across all three years (DA, 2018).

Studies Involving Nonpsychological (Other) Screeners That Could Reduce Initial Training Attrition Among All Recruits

3.11: Expanded Enlistment Eligibility Metrics (EEEM): Recommendations on a Non-Cognitive Screen for New Soldier Selection (Assembling Objects, WPA Dimensions, WPA Facets) (Knapp and Hefner, 2010)

Description of the Study

The purpose of this study was to provide recommendations to the Army on experimental non-cognitive predictor measures that could enhance entry-level soldier selection and classification decisions. The AFQT is a useful screener for selecting new soldiers; this study was designed to identify additional metrics, particularly those that identify noncognitive attributes, such as temperament, interests, and values, that could potentially be used to augment the AFQT. The EEEM project focuses on initial soldier selection. This EEEM study uses a subset of the Army Class data.

The report displays the incremental validity of several screeners in predicting six-month attrition over an AFQT-only model. Each screener-AFQT combination was compared with AFQT-only results. Six different screeners (AIM, TAPAS, RBI, Assembling Objects, WPA Dimensions, and WPA Facets) showed statistically significant improvements over AFQT alone. In this write-up, we present the results for Assembling Objects, WPA Dimensions, and WPA Facets. AIM, TAPAS, and RBI were covered in section 3.2 above.

RAND Arroyo Center Analysis

Potential cost avoidance was based on the estimated percentage point reduction in attrition from the potential inclusion of these screeners in the selection and classification process. The effect sizes were the incremental validity of each screener (reported as the change in Nagelkerke's R over the AFQT-only model), times the standard deviation of six-month attrition. The changes in R reported were 0.066 for Assembling Objects, 0.096 for WPA Dimensions, and 0.133 for WPA Facets. The potential annual accessions saved statistics are calculated by multiplying the effect sizes by Z_x (to remove the lowest 10 percent of scorers on the screening measure) by annual accessions. The cost of an IET graduate was multiplied by potential annual accessions saved to estimate potential annual costs avoided for each screener. Table 3.12 summarizes the key information.

Table 3.12. Potential Annual Costs Avoided from Using a Noncognitive Screen for New Soldier Selection—Assembling Objects, WPA Dimensions, WPA Facets

Screener	Effect Size ($RxSD_y$)	Z_x	Annual Accessions	Potential Annual Accessions Saved	Recruiting and Training Costs	Potential Annual Costs Avoided
Assembling Objects	2.11% [0.96%, 3.26%]	0.195	70,000	288 [131, 445]	$75,638	$21.8M [$10.0M, $33.7M]
WPA Dimensions	3.07% [1.92%, 4.22%]	0.195	70,000	419 [262, 576]	$75,638	$31.7M [$19.9M, $43.6M]
WPA Facets	4.26% [3.11%, 5.41%]	0.195	70,000	581 [425, 737]	$75,638	$44.0M [$32.1M, $55.8M]

SOURCES: Study documented in Deidre J. Knapp and Tonia S. Heffner, *Expanded Enlistment Eligibility Metrics (EEEM): Recommendations on a Non-Cognitive Screen for New Soldier Selection*, U.S. Army Research Institute for the Behavioral and Social Sciences, 2010. Recruiting and training costs derived from ATRRS and HQDA G-1, FY 2018.

3.12: Attrition in the Army from the Signing of the Enlistment Contract Through 180 Days of Service (Fischl and Blackwell, 2000)

Description of the Study

The objective of this study was to use data routinely collected by the time an enlisted contract is signed to identify predictors of IET attrition through 180 days. The data sample used consisted of nearly 160,000 non–prior service Regular Army contracts executed in FYs 1992 and 1993, tracked through FY 1995. This sample was split into two groups. The first group of contracts was used to identify screening predictors of attrition. Potential independent variables included, for example, AFQT category, high school diploma, weight, MOS, geographical area of contract, participation in a military youth program, college credits, and age. The regression results from the first sample were used to predict 180-day attrition in the second group of contracts, the holdout sample.

When individuals were outside the preferred recruitment group (i.e., those who had a high school diploma (Tier 1), were within weight standards, and scored in AFQT categories I–IIIB), those participating in military youth programs or having 15+ college credits had a lower attrition rate (15.97 percent) than those who did not (19.37 percent), although not as low as that for the preferred high school–diploma group (13.11 percent). Table 3.13 shows these results.

Table 3.13. Summary of Attrition Rates by Recruitment Group

Group Description	Number Enlisting	Number Attriting	Attrition Rate (%)
(1) Has a high school diploma, scored in AFQT Categories I–IIIB, and weighed less than 211 and 165 pounds for males and females, respectively	60,018	7,867	13.11
(2) Those who failed one or more of the criteria in the first group but with at least 15 college credits or participation in military youth groups that met other criteria	1,935	309	15.97
(3) All others who did not reach either of the specified criteria	7,162	1,387	19.37
Total	69,115	9,563	13.84

SOURCE: The numbers in this table come directly from Fischl and Blackwell, 2000.

RAND Arroyo Center Analysis

We first applied the principle of never allowing more than 10 percent of those who enter training to be non-Tier 1. We thus trimmed the original non–high school sample to ensure that these individuals constituted no more than 10 percent of the total. This involved proportionally decreasing groups 2 and 3 in Table 3.13 so that the sum amounted to 10 percent of the total sample. Table 3.14 lays out the adjusted sample.

Table 3.14. Derivation of the Modified Composition of Recruit Groups

Group Description	Number Enlisting	Number Attriting	Attrition Rate (%)
(1) Has a high school diploma	60,018	7,867	13.11
(2) Non–high school graduate but meet extra criteria	1,419	227	15.97
(3) Non–high school graduate and do not meet extra criteria	5,250	1,017	19.37
Total	66,687	9,111	13.66

We then resized the sample to 70,000 (see Table 3.15) to be roughly consistent with FY 2018 accessions into the Army. The overall attrition rate remained at 13.66 percent, and non–high school groups still amounted to only 10 percent of the total.

We then endeavored to reduce recruiting and IET training costs by screening out the entire highest attrition group (group 3) and proportionately redistributed the 7.9 percent of accessions to other groups. The results are shown in Table 3.15. Note that we were not able to screen out, as has been our convention, a full 10 percent of the sample because the higher attrition group was not large enough.

Table 3.15. Resized Recruit Groups After Eliminating Highest Attrition Group

Group Description	Number Enlisting	Number Attriting	Attrition Rate (%)
(1) Has high school diploma	68,384	8,965	13.11
(2) Non–high school graduate but meet extra criteria	1,616	258	15.97
(3) Non–high school graduate and do not meet extra criteria	0	0	0.00
Total	70,000	9,223	13.18

We then calculated the change in the overall attrition rate as 0.48 percentage point (13.66 percent minus 13.18 percent), and the number of IET graduates potentially saved was estimated at 341 (0.48 percent times 70,000, or, more precisely, 9,564 minus 9,223). We multiplied the cost of an IET graduate by 341 accessions saved to estimate potential annual costs avoided. Table 3.16 summarizes the key information.

Table 3.16. Potential Annual Costs Avoided Due to Reduced Attrition in the Army from the Signing of the Enlistment Contract through 180 Days of Service

Screener	Reduction in Attrition	Annual Accessions	Potential Annual Accessions Saved	Recruiting and Training Costs	Potential Annual Costs Avoided
High school graduate or additional credentials for non–high school graduates	0.48%	70,000	341	$75,638	$25.8M

SOURCES: Study documented in M. A. Fischl and Deanne L. Blackwell, *Attrition in the Army from the Signing of the Enlistment Contract Through 180 Days of Service*, U.S. Army Research Institute for Behavioral and Social Sciences, 2000. Training costs from MPA, information paper 2018. Throughput data came from the ATRRS individual file and FY 2017 NPS accessions in Army files.
NOTE: The results in Table 3.16 are taken from population results reported by the study authors. Therefore, no standard error of measurement is involved, and confidence intervals do not apply.

Studies Involving Nonpsychological (Other) Screeners That Could Reduce Initial Training Attrition Among Certain MOSs

3.13: The Roles of Perseverance, Cognitive Ability, and Physical Fitness in U.S. Army Special Forces Assessment and Selection (Beal, 2010)

Description of the Study

This research investigates the potential of measures of cognitive ability, physical fitness and perseverance to increase the graduation rate for the SFAS course. The 824 SFAS candidates who participated in this research (four classes' worth, conducted between November 2008 and February 2009) completed a series of tests and events that measured these concepts, most just before SFAS began. The authors used the outcome results and logistic regression to determine the importance of the various measures in passing the SFAS course.

The findings showed that 298 of the SFAS candidates in the author's sample failed to successfully complete the training because of voluntary withdrawals. Another 66 withdrew because of medical issues, and 110 completed the SFAS training but were not selected for further SF qualification training. There were 350 SFAS graduates selected for further qualification training. Results showed that most of the selected tests and measures could be used to predict soldier success in SFAS but with varying degrees of usefulness. For use in screening for SFAS admission just before the beginning of the SFAS course, the Army Physical Fitness Test (APFT) score was found to be the most effective measure for predicting soldiers who would voluntarily withdraw from SFAS training (see page 10 of the study).

RAND Arroyo Center Analysis

We reduced SF recruiting and training costs (through the SFAS course) by screening on APFT scores, essentially increasing the required score to begin the course. We applied the attrition and selection results listed in the study for dropping those in the bottom 10 percent of APFT scores to the planned number of in-service Army SF recruits in 2013. We calculated the potential number of saved recruits and selectees, and then the estimated potential annual cost avoidance by multiplying the recruiting and training cost through SFAS by the number of potential SFAS trainees saved

More specifically, the author found that eliminating the bottom 10 percent of APFT scorers would reduce the number selected by 12. Incorporating these numbers into the 2013 planned number of recruits would reduce recruits by 194 and selectees by 28. There would be more than enough selectees remaining to replace the 28 lost. Thus, the savings in failures avoided would be the full 194 recruits. Alternatively, one could assume that 62 additional recruits would be needed to replace the 28 lost selectees. This could be thought of as holding selectee quality constant on other dimensions and would result in a savings of 132 recruits. Table 3.17 summarizes the key information.

Table 3.17. Potential Annual Costs Avoided Resulting from SFAS Success After APFT

Screener	Proportion of Potential Recruits Eliminated	Annual SFAS Starts	Potential SFAS Trainees Saved	Potential Selectees Replaced	Recruiting and Training Costs Through SFAS	Potential Annual Costs Avoided
APFT	10%	1938	194 [131, 257]	0	$41,155	$8.0M [$5.4M, $10.6M]
APFT	10%	1938	194 [131, 257]	62	$41,155	$5.4M [$3.7M, $7.2M]

SOURCES: Study documented in Scott A. Beal, *The Roles of Perseverance, Cognitive Ability, and Physical Fitness in U.S. Army Special Forces Assessment and Selection*, U.S. Army Research Institute, 2010. SFAS starts from SWCS information. Recruitment and training costs per graduate are derived in separate table. Primary sources are MPA, TRADOC, and ATRM-159 course reports, and the SORB.

3.14: Air Force Officer Qualifying Test (AFOQT): Predictors of Undergraduate Pilot Training and Undergraduate Navigator Training Success (Arth et al., 1990)

Description of the Study

This study assessed whether subtests and composites of the AFOQT were correlated with performance (pass or fail) in UPT and Undergraduate Navigator Training (UNT). The study reports that 79 percent of officers completed UPT, and 86 percent of officers completed UNT. In addition, the pilot composite of the AFOQT was statistically significantly correlated with passing UPT ($r = 0.21$), and the navigator-technical composite of the AFOQT was statistically significantly correlated with completion of UNT ($r = 0.21$).

RAND Arroyo Center Analysis

We used the pass rates reported above to calculate the standard deviation of each outcome and then multiplied by the correlation to estimate the effect sizes for UPT and UNT. We removed the bottom 10 percent of scorers on each of the composites and multiplied by the number of trainees, which produces the number of potential trainees saved. We multiplied the number of potential trainees saved by the cost of each training program.

As shown in Table 3.18, screening out the bottom 10 percent of scorers on the navigator-technical composite of the AFOQT results in approximately one-third of a UNT trainee saved each year, for a potential annual cost avoidance of $59,804. Screening out the bottom 10 percent of scorers on the pilot composite of the AFOQT results in about 1.81 UPT trainees saved per year, for a potential annual cost avoidance of $401,997.

Table 3.18. Potential Annual Cost Avoided Using the AFOQT to Screen for Undergraduate Pilot Training and Undergraduate Navigator Training

Outcome	Screener	Effect Size ($rxSD_y$)	Z_x	Annual Trainees	Potential Trainees Saved	Training Cost	Potential Annual Cost Avoided
UNT	AFOQT-Navigator-Technical	7.14% [4.54%, 9.74%]	0.195	25	0.35 [0.22, 0.48]	$171,816	$0.06M [$0.04M, $0.08M]
UPT	AFOQT-Pilot	8.61% [5.63%, 11.59%]	0.195	108	1.81 [1.18, 2.44]	$221,698	$0.4M [$0.3M, $0.5M]

SOURCES: Study documented in Thomas O. Arth, Kurt W. Steuck, Christopher T. Sorrentino, and Eugene F. Burke, *Air Force Officer Qualifying Test (AFOQT): Predictors of Undergraduate Pilot Training and Undergraduate Navigator Training Success*, Air Force Human Resources Laboratory, 1990.

NOTES: We calculated the cost of fixed-wing pilot training ($221,698). Air Force fixed-wing pilot training consists of 40 days of Initial Flight Screening, followed by approximately one year of SUPT or nine months for UNT. We prorated the full cost of pilot training to determine the cost of the navigator training. The number of annual trainees was estimated using DA FY 2019 budget estimates, which reported trainees in each year, FYs 2017–2019. We used the average across all three years (DA, 2018).

3.15: Air Force Officer Training School Selection System Validation (Cowan, Barrett, and Wegner, 1990)

Description of the Study

The purpose of this study was to examine the selection process used for Air Force Officer Training School, with the intent of identifying and validating component variables. One component of the validation involved assessing which variables (e.g., AFOQT scores, cumulative grade point average, work experience) were correlated with performance in (passing) UPT and UNT.

The authors reported a pass rate in UNT of 85 percent and a pass rate in UPT of 79 percent. In addition, they report zero-order correlations between AFOQT-Pilot (AFOQT-PILOT) and UPT completion (0.10) and between AFOQT-Navigator (AFOQT-NAVT) and UNT completion (0.20), both of which are statistically significant.

RAND Arroyo Center Analysis

We first calculated the effect size of AFOQT-PILOT and AFOQT-NAVT for UPT and UNT, respectively, as the standard error of the passing times the respective reported correlations. We then screened out the bottom 10 percent of scorers, as usual, and applied the new mean for the standardized normal distribution. We multiplied the effect size by Z_x and the number of annual trainees (25 for UNT and 108 for UPT, as described earlier). This produced the number of potential trainees saved in a year, which we multiplied by the cost of training to estimate potential annual costs avoided. Table 3.19 shows the relevant information.

Table 3.19. Potential Annual Cost Avoided Using AFOQT to Screen for Undergraduate Pilot Training and Undergraduate Navigator Training

Outcome	Screener	Effect Size ($rxSD_y$)	Z_x	Annual Trainees	Potential Trainees Saved	Training Cost	Potential Annual Cost Avoided
UNT	AFOQT-NAVT	7.14% [3.04%, 11.24%]	0.195	25	0.35 [0.15, 0.55]	$171,816	$0.06M [$0.02M, $0.09M]
UPT	AFOQT-PILOT	4.07% [1.70%, 6.44%]	0.195	108	0.86 [0.36, 1.36]	$221,698	$0.2M [$0.08M, $0.3M]

SOURCES: Study documented in Douglas K. Cowan, Linda E. Barrett, and Toni G. Wegner, *Air Force Officer Training School Selection System Validation*, Air Force Human Resources Lab, 1990.
NOTES: We calculated the cost of fixed-wing pilot training ($221,698). Air Force fixed-wing pilot and navigator training consists of 40 days of Initial Flight Screening, followed by approximately one year of SUPT for pilots (Korger, 2019) and 9 months of UNT for navigators (Ohm, 2009). We prorated the full cost of pilot training to

determine the cost of the navigator training. The number of annual trainees was estimated using DA FY 2019 budget estimates, which reported trainees in each year, FYs 2017–2019. We used the average across all three years (DA, 2018).

Studies Involving Physical Training Interventions That Could Reduce Initial Training Attrition Among All Recruits

3.16: Outcomes of Fort Jackson's Physical Training and Rehabilitation Program in Army Basic Combat Training: Return to Training, Graduation, and 2-Year Retention (Hauret et al., 2004)

Description of the Study

This study is an evaluation of a supervised rehabilitation program (Physical Training and Rehabilitation Program [PTRP]) at Ft. Jackson between 1998 and 2001 for its effectiveness in reducing BCT training failures. Begun in 1995, PTRP provided a rehabilitation program for those who incurred a traumatic fracture, stress fracture, or other disabling injury during BCT. While the nature of the rehabilitation was not described, it was reported that the average stay in the program was a little over 10 weeks. The study sought to examine the percentage that entered PTRP, the number that returned to training, and the number who graduated from BCT.

Between January 3, 1998, and July 24, 2001, a period of 3.57 years, 4,258 Ft. Jackson trainees entered PTRP, for an average of 1,193 per year.[3] Of those entering, the study reports the number who passed PTRP and returned to BCT and the BCT graduation rate among those who completed PTRP. Using this information, we calculated a 38.39 percent BCT graduation rate (458 per year). This study did not report the number of BCT trainees at Ft. Jackson during the years of the study, but Hauret et al., 2004, reported the number, by gender, in 1998 (20,858 male trainees and 11,393 female trainees) and the percentage of injured trainees who entered PTRP. Office of the Secretary of Defense, Directorate of Accession Policy, reports the number of accessions in each year, 1998–2001. We used these numbers (percent injured who entered PTRP, number of trainees, and number of accessions by year) to adjust the reported results to be more consistent with the current force (70,000 accessions).

RAND Arroyo Center Analysis

We estimated recruiting and BCT training cost savings by applying the PTRP program to 70,000 Army recruits. To calculate the potential annual cost avoidance from discontinuing the PTRP, we compared (in 2018 dollars) the cost of the PTRP given its size during the period of the study with the cost of accessing and training new recruits. We divided the analysis into the steps

[3] There were 71,733 accessions in 1998 and an average of 73,751 accessions over the 3.57 years that the study covered.

described in the following subsections, where step numbers ending in "a" are adjusted from 1998–2001 to reflect the Army's current accessions.

Compute the Number of Recruits Entering PTRP and Accessions Saved

In Table 3.20, we show the steps of using the information in the study to determine that, after adjusting 1998–2001 results to the Army's current force, an estimated average of 1,132 Active Component (AC) soldiers per year entered the PTRP, of whom an average of 435 per year (38.45 percent) eventually passed BCT.

Table 3.20. Derivation of the Number of AC Soldiers Entering the PTRP and Passing BCT

Item	Value	Steps in Calculation	Sources and Calculations
1	1,228	Number of men entering Ft. Jackson PTRP from January 3, 1998, through July 24, 2001 (3.57-year period)	pp. 562–563 of study
2	3,030	Number of women entering Ft. Jackson PTRP from January 3, 1998, through July 24, 2001 (3.57-year period)	pp. 562–563 of study
3	4,258	Total entering Ft. Jackson PTRP from January 3, 1998 through July 24, 2001 (3.57-year period)	(1) + (2)
4	1,193	Average number entering PTRP per year	(3) / 3.57
4a	1,132	Adjustment of item 4 for 70,000 accessions	70,000 × (4) / 73,751 (see fn. 2)
5	1.6%	Percentage of male recruits entering PTRP per year	p. 562 of study for 3% injury rate; Table 3 of Hauret et al., 2001, for proportion of injuries assigned to PTRP (53.1%)
6	7.2%	Percentage of female recruits entering PTRP per year	p. 562 of study for 12% injury rate; Table 3 of Hauret et al., 2001, for proportion of injuries assigned to PTRP (60.3%)
7	20,354	Number male recruits at Ft. Jackson per year	Number of men in Ft. Jackson BCT in 1998 from Hauret et al., 2001, adjusted to 70,000 accessions
8	11,118	Number female recruits at Ft. Jackson per year	Number of women in Ft. Jackson BCT in 1998 from Hauret et al., 2001, adjusted to 70,000 accessions
9	31,472	Total recruits at Ft. Jackson/year	(7) + (8)
10	1,156	Men in final sample	p. 563 of study
11	2,803	Women in final sample	p. 563 of study
12	571	Men who passed PTRP, went back to BCT (over 3.57 years)	Table 2, p. 564 of study, adjusted to 70,000 accessions
13	1,060	Women who passed PTRP, went back to BCT (over 3.57 years)	Table 2, p. 564 of study, adjusted to 70,000 accessions
14	90.4%	BCT grad rate among male PTRP grads (over 3.57 years)	p. 564 of study

Item	Value	Steps in Calculation	Sources and Calculations
15	87.6%	BCT grad rate among female PTRP grads (over 3.57 years)	p. 565 of study
16	145	Male BCT grads per year	(14) × (12) / 3.57
17	260	Female BCT grads per year	(15) × (13) / 3.57
18	435	Estimated number of accessions saved per year at Ft. Jackson	(3) × [(16) + (17)] / [(10) + (11)]
19	1.4%	Reduction in attrition percentage	(18) / (9)
20	38.45%	Reduction in attrition percentage for PTRP entrants	(18) / (4)

NOTE: At the time of data collection, 72 men and 227 women were still in the PTRP and were therefore excluded from the analyses.

Compute the Cost of the PTRP Compared to the Cost of Replacing with New BCT Recruits

We next estimated the cost of the PTRP program. Given we did not have access to the historical cost of the PTRP, we approximated the weekly cost of the program as being the same as the weekly cost for BCT. Table 3.21 shows the results.

Table 3.21. Estimation of the Cost of the PTRP Program

Item	Value	Steps in Calculation	Source/Calculation
1	$16,973	BCT cost per enrollee	Derived in Appendix A
2	63	Length of BCT (in days)	ATRRS
3	74	Length of PTRP (in days)	Weighted average of numbers in Table 1 of the study (p. 564)
4	1.17	Ratio of program lengths	(3) / (2)
5	$19,937	Estimated PTRP cost per enrollee	x (4)
6	1,132	Number of PTRP enrollees	Derived in table in Table 3.21 (4a)
6a	2,519	Number of PTRP enrollees for 70,000 accessions	(6) × 70,000 / 31,472
7	$22,574,505	Total cost of PTRP program	(6) × (5)
7a	$50,210,443	Total cost of PTRP program for 70,000 accessions	(6a) × (5)
8	435	Accessions saved at Ft. Jackson	Derived in Table 3.21 (18)
8a	968	Accessions saved for 70,000 accessions	(8) × 70,000 / 31,472
9	$47,430	BCT Recruiting and Training Costs per Replacement	Derived in Appendix A
10	$20,651,301	Potential costs avoided by replacing accessions saved at Ft. Jackson	(8) × (9)
10a	$45,932,833	Potential costs avoided by replacing accessions saved for 70,000 accessions	(10) × 70,000 / 31,472

Estimate the Potential Costs Avoided

We subtracted the net cost of the PTRP from the cost of the alternative strategy—replacing loses with new recruits—to arrive at an estimate of net savings from eliminating the PRPT. Table 3.22 summarizes the key information.

Table 3.22. Potential One-Time Cost Avoided Due to Discontinuing the PTRP

Intervention	Reduction in Attrition	Estimated Annual BCT Trainees	Potential Annual Accessions Saved	BCT Recruiting and Training Costs/ Replacement	Potential Costs Avoided by Accessions Saved	Number Entering PTRP Annually	PTRP Cost Per Enrollee	Cost of PTRP Program	Potential Annual Cost Avoided
PTRP	1.40%	70,000	968	$47,430	$45,932,833	2,519	$19,937	$50,210,443	($4.3M)

SOURCES: Study documented in Keith G. Hauret, Joseph J. Knapik, Jeffery L. Lange, Heidi A. Heckel, Dana L. Coval, and David H. Duplessis, "Outcomes of Fort Jackson's Physical Training and Rehabilitation Program in Army Basic Combat Training: Return to Training, Graduation, and 2-Year Retention," *Military Medicine*, Vol. 169, No. 7, July 2004. BCT Recruiting and training costs and replacement derived from ATRRS and HQDA G-1, FY 2018 data (see Appendix A). The number of BCT trainees and number of trainees with injuries who entered PTRP from Hauret et al., 2001. The average number of FY 1998–2001 annual accessions adjusted to 70,000 to reflect current accession requirements and used in estimates.
NOTE: The results in this table were taken from population results reported by the study authors. Therefore, no standard error of measurement is involved, and confidence intervals do not apply.

3.17: Retention in Service of Recruits Assigned to the Army Physical Fitness Test Enhancement Program in Basic Combat Training (Knapik et al., 2003)

Description of the Study

This study examined the success of the Army Physical Fitness Test Enhancement Program (APFTEP) at Ft. Jackson from January 1999 to June of 2001. BCT candidates were selected to go into the APFTEP at the end of basic training if they could not pass the final APFT but had otherwise qualified for graduation. The APFTEP provides both daily physical training and military training (the latter to sustain general knowledge and skills learned in BCT). Participants are given four to five weeks to pass the APFT, with weekly tests to determine if they have improved enough to qualify.

The study reported that 1,383 (about 2.75 percent of AC recruits) entered the APFTEP at Ft. Jackson between January 1999 and June 2001. Of those, 82.44 percent graduated from APFTEP and BCT. However, an additional 19.57 percent of those that entered APFTEP became part of one-year attrition and could arguably have failed their physical during AIT after passing APFTEP.

RAND Arroyo Center Analysis

The overall aim was to reduce recruiting and BCT training costs through the APFTEP program applied to 70,000 Army accessions. To estimate potential annual cost avoidance, we compared the cost of the scope of a 2018 APFTEP program with the cost of accessing and training new recruits. We added to the cost of APFTEP the cost of further training for those we considered *false positives*, defined as APTFEP graduates who nonetheless ended up failing the physical during their first year. The analysis can be divided into the steps described in the following subsections.

Compute the Number of Recruits Entering APFTEP and Accessions Saved

Table 3.23 shows the steps of estimating that 1,925 AC soldiers would enter the APFTEP if applied Army-wide to 70,000 accessions and if 1,311 accessions could be saved. Determining the latter number required that we subtract what we considered the false positives from the number of APFTEP graduates. This provides a generous estimate of the number of false positives because there is about a 6-percent attrition rate between training completion and the end of the first year; thus, not all the additional APFTEP attrition is likely to be related to APFT.

Table 3.23. Derivation of the Number of AC Soldiers Who Enter APFTEP and Number of Accessions Saved

Item	Value	Steps in Calculation	Source/Calculation
1	637	Number of men entering Ft. Jackson APFTEP from January 1999–June 2001	First page of study (p. 490)
2	746	Number of women entering Ft. Jackson APFTEP from January 1999–June 2001	First page of study (p. 490)
3	35,750	Number of men entering Ft. Jackson from January 1999–June 2001	Table 1 of study (p. 492)
4	24,592	Number of women entering Ft. Jackson from January 1999–June 2001	Table 1 of study (p. 492)
5	1.78%	APFTEP participation rate among men at Ft. Jackson	(1) / (3)
6	3.03%	APFTEP participation rate among women men at Ft. Jackson	(2) / (4)
7	1.99%	Gender-weighted APFTEP participation rate at Ft. Jackson	
8	70,000	IET inputs for AC Army	
9	83.25%	Estimated portion of IET inputs for AC Army that are men	FY 2017 Population Representation in the Military Services, Table B-1
10	16.75%	Estimated portion of IET inputs for AC Army that are women	FY 2017 Population Representation in the Military Services, Table B-1
11	1,038	Number of men entering APFTEP, scaled to 70,000	(8) × (9) × (5)
12	356	Number of women entering APFTEP, scaled to 70,000	(8) × (10) × (6)
13	74%	Portion of men who participated in APFTEP who were retained in service over a one-year period	Figure 3 in study (p. 491)
14	63%	Portion of women who participated in APFTEP who were retained in service over a one-year period	Figure 3 in study (p. 491)
15	72.16%	Gender-weighted portion who participated in APFTEP who were retained in service over a one-year period	(9) × (13) + (10) × (14)
16	768	Estimated number of men saved by participating in APFTEP	(11) × (13)
17	224	Estimated number of women saved by participating in APFTEP	(12) × (14)
18	992	Estimated number of men and women saved by participating in APFTEP	
19	3.3	Difference in one-year survival rate post-BCT between APFTEP participants and nonparticipants-men	BCT graduation rates on p. 491 less survival difference between program participants and nonparticipants at 1 year
20	1	Difference in one-year survival rate post-BCT between APFTEP participants and nonparticipants—women	BCT graduation rates on p. 491 less survival difference between program participants and nonparticipants at 1 year

Item	Value	Steps in Calculation	Source/Calculation
21	25	Additional number of BCT graduates lost by end of first year relative to nonparticipants—men	(16) × (19)
22	2.24	Additional number of BCT graduates lost by end of first year relative to nonparticipants—women	(17) × (20)

SOURCE: CNA, 2017, Table B-1.

Compute the Net Cost of the APFTEP

We next estimated the cost of the APFTEP program. Given that we did not have access to the historical cost of the APFTEP, we approximated the weekly cost of the program as being the same as that cost for BCT. Table 3.24 shows the results.

Table 3.24. Estimation of the Cost of the APFTEP

Item	Value	Steps in Calculation	Source/Calculation
1	$16,973	BCT cost per enrollee	Derived in Appendix A
2	$31,350	AIT cost per enrollee	Derived in Appendix A
3	9	Length of BCT (in weeks)	ATRRS
4	4	Length of APFTEP (in weeks)	p. 490 of study
5	$7,544	Estimated APFTEP cost per enrollee	(1) × [(4) / (3)]
6	1,394	Number of APFTEP enrollees	Derived in Table 3.23
7	$10,516,283	Total cost of APFTEP	(6) × (5)
8	27	Estimated number of false positives	Derived in Table 3.23
9	$865,203	Estimated cost of training false positives	(8) × (2)
10	$11,381,486	Cost of the APFTEP Program Plus AIT Cost of False Positives	(9) + (7)

We subtracted the net cost of the APFTEP from the cost of the alternative strategy—replacing loses with new recruits—to arrive at a net cost of the intervention. Table 3.25 summarizes the key information.

Table 3.25. Potential Annual Cost Avoided Due to Saved Accessions from APFTEP

Intervention	APFTEP 1-Yr Survival %	Annual Accessions	Percent Entering APFTEP	Number Entering APFTEP	Potential Accessions Saved	Recruiting and BCT Costs per Replacement	Potential Recruiting and BCT Costs Avoided	APFTEP Program Cost	Cost of APFTEP Program Plus AIT Cost for False Positives	Potential Annual Cost Avoided[a]
APFTEP	72.16	70,000	1.99%	1,394	992	$47,430	$47,071,472	$10,516,283	$11,381,486	$35.7M

SOURCES: Study documented in Joseph J. Knapik, Keith G. Hauret, Jeffery L. Lange, and Brian Jovag, "Retention in Service of Recruits Assigned to the Army Physical Fitness Test Enhancement Program in Basic Combat Training," *Military Medicine*, Vol. 168, No. 6, June 2003. Number of recruits entering BCT and OSUT during 2014 are from ATRRS. Recruiting and training costs are from MPA, modified in cost of training section.
NOTES: The results in Table 3.27 are taken from population results reported by the study authors. Therefore, no standard error of measurement is involved, and confidence intervals do not apply. Figures adjusted to reflect recent gender split and 70,000 accessions.
[a] Using APFTEP versus replacing with new accessions.

3.18: Evaluation of Two Army Fitness Programs: The TRADOC Standardized Physical Training Program for Basic Combat Training and the Fitness Assessment Program (Discharges Among Standardized Group Participants) (Knapik, Darakjy, et al., 2004)

Description of the Study

To attempt to improve fitness and reduce injuries and attrition from BCT, the Army developed a standardized physical training program. This study evaluated the effectiveness of the program by comparing two groups, the standardized group (SG) that implemented the new training program and the nonstandardized group (NSG) that implemented the traditional BCT physical training program. This study also evaluated the Fitness Assessment Program (FAP), a program designed to train new recruits who fail a basic fitness test at the reception station until they can pass the test and enter BCT. The design of the study included five BCT companies that implemented the SG and five that performed the traditional BCT physical training program. Among recruits who failed the fitness test at the reception station, some trained in the FAP (FAP Control) and some entered BCT without entering the FAP (FAP Test). The analysis that follows is about BCT discharges among SG and non-SG participants. Study 3.19 evaluated discharges among FAP Control and FAP Test participants. A study we discuss later, 7.3, analyzed injury rates among members of the SG and NSG. (There were no statistically significant differences in injury rates between members of the FAP Test and FAP Control groups, so that outcome is not presented in this report.)

There were no significant differences between the SG and NSG in the proportion of men (NSG = 93 percent, SG = 94 percent) or women (NSG = 89.2 percent, SG = 86.9 percent) who completed BCT. This implies that the Army should not implement the new standardized training program for BCT if it has an incremental cost.

RAND Arroyo Center Analysis

Potential costs avoided were based on the cost of training for drill instructors involved in the standardized training program. These costs involved the two-day training requirement reported in the study. As discussed in Chapter 2, we estimated the daily cost of this training as $1,046 using FY 2017 ATRM-159. As also discussed in Chapter 2, we assumed a trainer-to-soldier ratio of 1:20 for BCT but assumed that a drill sergeant can train four BCT classes per year, making the ratio 1:80.

Participants in the SG were not statistically significantly less likely to be discharged from BCT, so the potential annual costs avoided come from not implementing the SG for BCT and, therefore, eliminating the costs associated with running the program. That results in $1,872,545 in savings (adjusted for inflation) associated with not implementing the SG for a cohort of 70,000 accessions. The results are taken from population results reported by the study authors.

Therefore, there is no standard error of measurement involved, and confidence intervals do not apply.

Study 7.3 analyzes cost savings resulting from lower injury rates among SG participants compared with NSG.

3.19: Evaluation of Two Army Fitness Programs: The TRADOC Standardized Physical Training Program for Basic Combat Training and the Fitness Assessment Program (Discharges Among Fitness Assessment Program Participants) (Knapik, Darakjy, et al., 2004)

Description of the Study

To reduce injuries and attrition from BCT, the Army developed the FAP. This study evaluated the effectiveness of the program by comparing two groups among those who failed the initial fitness test administered at the reception battalion: a test group that did not receive FAP training and a control group that received FAP training.

Among study participants, 8.18 percent of men and 18.60 percent of women participated in FAP. For men, the BCT discharge rate among FAP Test participants was 18.8 percent, compared with 6.3 percent for the FAP Control group. Among women, the discharge rate among FAP Test participants was 21.9 percent, compared with 11.7 percent for the FAP Control group. The differences were marginally significant. The differences in completing training in the same unit one started BCT with were highly significant. We report the rates for discharges because they are a more complete measure of BCT success.

RAND Arroyo Center Analysis

We first scaled FAP participation rates to a 70,000-person accession cohort. Using the gender distribution reported in the FY 2017 Population Representation report (see Chapter 2), the gender-weighted FAP participation rate became 9.92 percent. Next, we calculated the difference in discharge rates between the FAP test and control groups. For men, the difference was 12.5 percentage points, and for women, the difference was 10.2 percentage points. The gender-weighted difference in discharge rates between the two groups is 12.11 percentage points. We multiplied the percentage point difference in discharge rates by the estimated number of FAP participants in a 70,000-person accession cohort to estimate the number of BCT discharges saved.

FAP training takes approximately two weeks during BCT. To calculate program costs, we multiply the cost of a BCT enrollee ($16,973) by 2 / 9 because BCT was nine weeks, or $3,771.78 per FAP participant.

Applying a 12.11-percentage point reduction in BCT discharges to the estimated number of FAP participants, we estimated potential annual accessions saved of 841, resulting in potential recruiting and BCT costs avoided of $39,908,778. We then subtracted the FAP program cost of

$26,196,493 ($3,771.78 per participant multiplied by 70,000 × 0.0992 participants). The resulting estimated potential annual costs avoided are $13,712,284, as shown in Table 3.26.

Table 3.26. Potential Annual Cost Avoided Due to Participation in the Fitness Assessment Program

Intervention	Reduction in Attrition	FAP Participation Rate	Annual Accessions	Potential Accessions Saved	Recruiting and BCT Costs per Replacement	Potential Recruiting and BCT Costs Avoided	FAP Program Cost	Potential Annual Cost Avoided
FAP	12.11%	9.92	70,000	841	$47,430	$39,908,778	$26,196,493	$13.7M

SOURCES: Study documented in Knapik, Joseph J., Salima Darakjy, Shawn Scott, Keith G. Hauret, Sara Canada, Roberto Marin, Frank Palkoska, Steven VanCamp, Eugene Piskator, William Rieger, and Bruce H. Jones, *Evaluation of Two Army Fitness Programs: The TRADOC Standardized Physical Training Program for Basic Combat Training and the Fitness Assessment Program*, Army Center for Health Promotion and Preventive Medicine, February 2004.
NOTE: The results in this table are taken from population results reported by the study authors. Therefore, there is no standard error of measurement involved, and confidence intervals do not apply.

Chapter 4. First-Term Attrition

This chapter presents information on the potential annual costs avoided from lowering first-term attrition through the use of personality tests or other screeners. Table 4.1 categorizes the studies considered in this chapter, providing full titles and assigning study numbers.

Unless otherwise indicated, all effect sizes are in percentage points.

Table 4.1. First-Term Attrition Studies

Study Number	**Name of Study**
Studies Involving Personality Tests or Screeners That Could Reduce First-Term Attrition	
4.1	Setting Enlistment Standards on The ABLE To Reduce Attrition (White, Nord, and Mael, 1990)
4.2	Tier One Performance Screen Initial Operational Test and Evaluation: 2012 Annual Report (Knapp and LaPort, 2014)
Studies Involving the Use of Other Survey-based Screeners to Reduce First-Term Attrition	
4.3	Relations Between Select21 Predictor Measures and First-Term Attrition (Putka and Bradley, 2008)
4.4	The Optimal Job-Person Match Case for Attrition Reduction (Greenston, 1997)
Studies Involving Nonpsychological (Other) Screeners to Reduce First-Term Attrition	
4.5	A Longitudinal Examination of First Term Attrition and Reenlistment Among FY 1999 Enlisted Accessions (Strickland, 2005)
4.6	What Characterizes Successful Enlistees in the All-Volunteer Force: A Study of Male Recruits in the U.S. Navy (Cooke and Quester, 1992)
4.7	First-Term Attrition in the Navy: Causes and Proposed Solutions (Larson and Kewley, 2000)
Studies Involving Nonpsychological (Other) Screeners to Reduce First-Term Attrition Among Certain MOSs	
4.8	Soldier Selection: Past, Present, and Future (Zook, 1996)

NOTE: ABLE = Assessment of Background and Life Experiences.

Studies Involving Personality Tests or Screeners That Could Reduce First-Term Attrition

4.1: Setting Enlistment Standards on the ABLE to Reduce Attrition (White, Nord, and Mael, 1990)

Description of the Study

This study examined the incremental validity of the ABLE as a predictor of, and potential screener for, first-term attrition at 21 months. The ABLE measure is a 199-item temperament scale that was previously validated as part of the Army's Project A efforts. ABLE includes a number of subscales (commonly reported composites are Achievement, Discipline, and Stress Tolerance), as well as validation subscales. The concurrent validation effort, focusing on the prediction of military personnel's job performance, used a 70 item (Form A) subset of the ABLE.

The results used for the present analyses were extracted from the second Project A validation effort, a longitudinal evaluation of the ABLE measure, which focused on attrition and first-term reenlistment. Soldiers completed the ABLE measure as part of a battery of new cognitive and noncognitive tests during the longitudinal validation phase. The sample consisted of first-term soldiers across 21 MOS classifications (N = 42,733).

Attrition was defined as separation before completing 21 months of service. Given this dichotomous operationalization of attrition, this study used a logistic regression model assessing ABLE's incremental prediction of first-term attrition (at 21 months) over sex, race, length of time (months) in delayed entry program, high school diploma graduation, General Educational Development (GED), combat MOS versus noncombat MOS, raw AFQT scores (continuous), and two-year enlistment versus other than two-year enlistment. Independent effects of these demographic variables were provided along with the screener variable of interest (ABLE) as logistic regression model coefficients (Table 3, p. 524). The reported logistic regression coefficient for ABLE was –0.0517, after controlling for the previously identified predictors.

RAND Arroyo Center Analysis

Potential cost avoidance was operationalized as the recruiting and IET training costs reduced by using ABLE to screen out the 10 percent of accessions at highest risk for attrition according to the ABLE measure. Cost avoidance was estimated as the absolute number of attrition losses avoided and the total dollar value of recruiting and IET training costs avoided by eliminating this number of attrition losses.

To illustrate how ABLE would likely function as a screener, its coefficient must be transformed into ABLE's effect on reducing losses among first-term enlistees who would otherwise attrit by 21 months. The following paragraphs describe the specifics of applying this procedure to the study's findings.

First, the logistic regression coefficient was multiplied by percentiles 1–100, and the products were summed. The sum was then divided by 100, producing a mean value of –2.61085. Next, this procedure was repeated for percentiles 1–100 and divided by 90, yielding a mean value of –2.86935. The percentage point decrease in attrition was then estimated as

$$\exp(-2.61085) / [1+\exp(-2.61085)] - \exp(-2.86935) / [1+\exp(-2.86935)] = -0.014754,$$

that is, –1.4754 percentage points.

Once this percentage point reduction in attrition had been calculated, it was applied to an active component recruitment number of 70,000. Because ABLE's initial validation and attrition sample consisted of soldiers across MOS classifications and would be used regardless of MOS, the potential savings in recruiting and IET training costs were estimated using the entire accession population.

Cost savings represented eliminating the recruiting and IET training costs that would otherwise be spent on the losses avoided by using ABLE. The cost was estimated to be $75,638 per IET graduate, as discussed in Appendix A. This study suggests that 1,033 accessions could be saved per year by using ABLE to screen out high-risk accessions. Accordingly, a total of $78,115,940 in recruiting and training costs could potentially be avoided annually. Table 4.2 summarizes the key information.

Table 4.2. Potential Annual Costs Avoided Due to Reduced Attrition from Using ABLE as a Screener

Screener	Reduction in Attrition	Annual Accessions	Potential Annual Accessions Saved	Recruiting and Training Costs	Potential Annual Costs Avoided
ABLE	1.48% [1.46%, 1.50%]	70,000	1,033 [1,016, 1,050]	$75,638	$78.1M [$76.9M, $79.4M]

SOURCES: Study documented in L. A. White, R. D. Nord, and F. A. Mael, *Setting Enlistment Standards on the ABLE to Reduce Attrition*, Army Research Institute, 1990. Recruiting and training costs derived from G-1 and ATRRS, FY 2018.

4.2: Tier One Performance Screen Initial Operational Test and Evaluation: 2012 Annual Report (Knapp and LaPort, 2014)

Description of the Study

This is an annual report from an initial operational test and evaluation of the TAPAS. As mentioned in previous studies, the AFQT is a primary metric for selecting soldiers. There was a desire to evaluate other metrics, particularly those that screen for noncognitive attributes, such as temperament, values, and interests. Several different metrics were selected for examination in previous studies; the Army selected the TAPAS to be the basis of an initial test and evaluation of the Tier One Performance Screen.

The study reports the improvement in prediction of 30-month attrition from a model that includes the AFQT score only to a model that includes both the AFQT and the TAPAS scores—reported as a change in R (0.03). There were also significant improvements in the prediction of attrition for the AFQT + TAPAS model for 24 month, 12-month, and 6-month attrition.

RAND Arroyo Center Analysis

The potential costs avoided were based on the percentage reduction in attrition from the inclusion of the TAPAS screener in the selection process. The effect size was the change in R between the two models (0.03) times the standard deviation of the 30-month attrition rate shown in Table 2.1. This effect size was multiplied by Z_x to remove the bottom 10 percent of the screener score distribution. Using the cost of an IET graduate, we calculated potential annual costs avoided as $13,728,956. Table 4.3 summarizes the key information.

Table 4.3. Potential Annual Costs Avoided from Using TAPAS as a Screener

Screener	Effect Size ($RxSD_y$)	Z_x	Annual Accessions	Potential Annual Accessions Saved	Recruiting and Training Costs	Potential Annual Costs Avoided
TAPAS	1.33% [0.03%, 2.63%]	0.195	70,000	182 [4, 360]	$75,638	$13.7M [$0.3M, $27.1M]

SOURCES: Study documented in Deidre. J. Knapp and Kate A. LaPort, eds., *Tier One Performance Screen Initial Operational Test and Evaluation: 2012 Annual Report*, U.S. Army Research Institute for the Behavioral and Social Sciences, 2014. Recruiting and training costs derived from HQDA G-1 and ATRRS, FY 2018.

Studies Involving the Use of Other Survey-Based Screeners to Reduce First-Term Attrition

4.3: Relations Between Select21 Predictor Measures and First-Term Attrition (Putka and Bradley, 2008)

Description of the Study

This study examined a collection of measures of individual differences, the Select21 predictor measures, concerning the successful selection, accession, and job classification of future entry-level soldiers. The Select21 predictor measures were also used to predict attrition, from initial entry into the Army through 15 months. The report includes findings from three waves of data collection conducted by ARI: pilot test (September–November 2003), faking research (January–February 2004), and field test (August–September 2004). The attrition data included in the report extend through 15 months. These results were used to explore potential measures used for selection of soldiers more likely to complete their service obligations.

Attrition was defined as separation before completing 15 months of service. The Select21 predictor measures examined in the study comprised seven tests predicting attrition. The effects of the Select21 predictor measures on 15-month attrition were reported as independent zero-order correlations for each of the seven measures, as follows: Army Beliefs Survey ($r = 0.16$, Table 25, p. 33), Psychomotor Tests Composite ($r = 0.075$, Table 9, p. 10), RBI ($r = 0.24$, Table 12, p. 14), Work Suitability Inventory ($r = 0.15$, Table 14, p. 17), Work Preferences Survey ($r = 0.14$, Table 18, p. 23), Pre-Service Expectations Survey ($r = 0.06$, Table 20, p. 26), and Work Values Inventory ($r = 0.10$, Table 22, p. 29). An additional screener, the Predictor Situational Judgment Test, was not included because it displayed a nonsignificant, negative relationship with attrition.

RAND Arroyo Center Analysis

Potential cost avoidance was operationalized as the recruiting and IET training costs avoided by using the Select21 predictor measures to screen out the 10 percent of accessions at highest risk for attrition. It was estimated using the absolute number of potential attrition losses avoided times the cost per IET graduate, i.e., the total dollar value of recruiting and training costs avoided by eliminating this number of attrition losses.

The zero-order correlations with the 15-month attrition rate (17.88 percent, based on Table 2.1) were multiplied by the standard deviation of that rate to estimate the effect size. Next, the effect size was multiplied by Z_x to reflect screening out the bottom 10 percent of the distribution. The result was applied to 70,000 accessions to estimate the annual number of accessions saved, because initial development and validation of the Select21 predictor measures consisted of a diverse sample of soldiers and these screeners would be used across MOS classifications. Potential annual cost avoidance represented eliminating the recruiting and IET training costs that would otherwise be spent replacing these losses.

This study suggests that 314 to 1,255 accessions might be saved per year by using the Select21 predictor measures to screen out high-risk accessions. Accordingly, estimated total recruiting and training potential costs avoided range between $23,738,349 and $94,953,397 annually. Table 4.4 summarizes the key information for each of the Select21 predictor measures.

Table 4.4. Potential Annual Costs Avoided Due to Reduced Attrition from Using Select21 as a Screener

Screener	Effect Size ($rxSD_y$)	Z_x	Annual Accessions	Potential Annual Accessions Saved	Recruiting and Training Costs	Potential Annual Costs Avoided
Army Beliefs Survey	6.13% [3.02%, 9.24%]	0.195	70,000	837 [412, 1,262]	$75,638	$63.3M [$31.2M, $95.4M]
Psychomotor Tests Composite	2.87% [-0.40%, 6.14%]	0.195	70,000	392 [–54.69, 839]	$75,638	$29.7M [-$4.1M, $63.5M]
RBI	9.2% [6.52%, 11.88%]	0.195	70,000	1,255 [890, 1,620]	$75,638	$95.0M [$67.3M, $122.6M]
Work Suitability Inventory	5.75% [3.00%, 8.50%]	0.195	70,000	785 [410, 1,160]	$75,638	$59.3M [$31.0M, $87.7M]
Work Preferences Survey	5.36% [2.89%, 7.83%]	0.195	70,000	732 [395, 1,069]	$75,638	$55.4M [$29.9M, $80.9M]
Pre-Service Expectations Survey	2.3% [–0.79%, 5.39%]	0.195	70,000	314 [–108, 736]	$75,638	$23.7M [–$8.2M, $55.7M]
Work Values Inventory	3.83% [1.15%, 6.51%]	0.195	70,000	523 [156, 890]	$75,638	$39.6M [$11.8M, $67.3M]

SOURCES: Study documented in Dan J. Putka and Kevin M. Bradley, *Relations Between Select21 Predictor Measures and First-Term Attrition*, Army Research Institute, 2008. Recruiting and training costs derived from HQDA G-1 and ATRRS, FY 2018.
NOTE: Because each Select21 predictor measure was reported independently and because no intercorrelations among these measures were reported, each of the Select21 predictor measures was treated separately for these cost savings analyses. Thus, it is unknown how these potentially intercorrelated measures may be used in combination to avoid recruiting and IET training costs. RBI, as developed by ARI, consists of personality measures, although biodata inventories more generally include experience and other factors.

4.4: The Optimal Job-Person Match Case for Attrition Reduction (Greenston, 1997)

Description of the Study

The objective of this study was to examine an interaction between personal characteristics and organizational factors as they affect first-term attrition. Specifically, the study used regression to look at the association between attrition behavior and predicted job performance. The magnitude of this relationship was then used to estimate the attrition reduction that could be had by improving job-person match using the Enlisted Personnel Allocation System (EPAS). This attrition reduction was used to estimate cost savings in terms of reduced recruiting and training costs if the EPAS were to be implemented.

This study reports the potential reduction in 36-month attrition of optimized job-person match using EPAS. The predicted number of losses saved (368) for the 1991 cohort (78,241 accessions) represents 0.47 percent of accessions.

RAND Arroyo Center Analysis

We rescaled the number using the ratio of 70,000 accessions to 1991 accessions, which resulted in an estimate of 329 losses saved. We then estimated potential annual costs avoided as the cost of recruiting and producing an IET graduate times 329. Table 4.5 presents the key information.

Table 4.5 Potential Annual Costs Avoided Due to Reduced Attrition from Using EPAS in Job-Person Matches

Screener	Reduction in Attrition	Annual Accessions	Potential Annual Accessions Saved	Recruiting and Training Costs	Potential Annual Costs Avoided
Job-Person Match	0.47% [0.03%, 0.91%]	70,000	329 [21, 637]	$75,638	$24.2M [$1.6M, $46.9M]

SOURCES: Study documented in Peter M. Greenston, *The Optimal Job-Person Match Case for Attrition Reduction*, U.S. Army Research Institute for the Behavioral and Social Sciences, 1997. Recruiting and training costs derived from HQDA G-1 and ATRRS, FY 2018.

Studies Involving Nonpsychological (Other) Screeners to Reduce First-Term Attrition

4.5: A Longitudinal Examination of First Term Attrition and Reenlistment Among FY 1999 Enlisted Accessions (Strickland, 2005)

Description of the Study

Project First Term was a longitudinal study conducted by ARI to evaluate models of attrition based on information available from the TAPDB. This research effort examined information that is routinely available from personnel records at the time soldiers enter the Army that may also be used to predict IET attrition. The sample comprised enlisted soldiers from the FY 1999 cohort through their first term of service. The study's time points included attrition at every stage of soldiers' first term of enlistment and up to a period of 48 months of service and reenlistment, including entrance into the service, completing training segments, conducting duty assignments, and leaving the service.

Attrition was defined as separation before completing 48 months of service. This study reported adjusted correlations among alternative decisions regarding use of commonly collected information about recruits available from TAPDB—education tier, high-quality recruit status, and AFQT category. The alternatives provided estimated reductions in attrition attributable to the alternative uses of these predictors of attrition (see study Table 3.6, p. 61).

RAND Arroyo Center Analysis

Potential cost avoidance was operationalized as the recruiting and IET training costs avoided by using the top pretraining predictors of attrition to screen out 10 percent of accessions at highest risk for attrition. It was estimated as the absolute number of attrition losses avoided multiplied by the dollar value of recruiting and IET training costs avoided for an IET graduate. The effect of using TAPDB information was reported as adjusted correlations with 48-month attrition: education tier without high school diploma (adj. $r = 0.12$); AFQT category, not in AFQT Category I, II, or IIIA (adj. $r = 0.06$); or not high-quality recruit, i.e., in one or both of the preceding groups (adj. $r = 0.07$). The study's adjusted correlations were multiplied by the standard deviation of attrition at 48 months (rate reported in Table 2.1). Next, this effect size was multiplied by Z_x to screen out the bottom 10 percent of the accessions for each screener. This provided an estimated annualized number of accessions saved. Potential cost avoidance represented eliminating the recruiting and IET training costs that would otherwise be spent on these losses. Table 4.6 presents the key results.

Table 4.6. Potential Annual Costs Avoided Due to Reduced Attrition from Using Education, AFQT Category, and High-Quality Recruit Indicators as Screeners

Screener	Effect Size ($rxSD_y$)	Z_x	Annual Accessions	Potential Annual Accessions Saved	Recruiting and Training Costs	Potential Annual Costs Avoided
Education Tier = 2[a]	5.79% [5.41%, 6.17%]	0.195	70,000	790 [738, 842]	$75,638	$59.8M [$55.8M, $63.7M]
AFQT Category (<I–IIIA)[b]	2.89% [2.51%, 3.27%]	0.195	70,000	394 [342, 446]	$75,638	$29.8M [$25.9M, $33.8M]
Non–High-Quality Recruit[c]	3.38% [3.00%, 3.76%]	0.195	70,000	461 [409, 513]	$75,638	$34.9M [$30.4M, $38.9M]

SOURCES: Study documented in William J. Strickland, *A Longitudinal Examination of First Term Attrition and Reenlistment Among FY1999 Enlisted Accessions*, U.S. Army Research Institute for the Behavioral and Social Sciences, 2005. Recruiting and training costs derived from HQDA G-1 and ATRRS, FY 2018.

[a] Education tier was classified using the Army's three education categories: Tier 1 recruits are high school diploma graduates or equivalent; Tier 2 recruits do not have a traditional high school diploma but do have an alternative education credential (mostly GED); and Tier 3 recruits are non–high school graduates with no alternative credential.

[b] AFQT Category included I, II, IIIA, IIIB, and IV.

[c] High-quality recruits are high school diploma holders who score at or above the 50th percentile on the AFQT.

4.6: What Characterizes Successful Enlistees in the All-Volunteer Force: A Study of Male Recruits in the U.S. Navy (Cooke and Quester, 1992)

Description of the Study

This study explores the relationship between career outcomes (e.g., completion of obligated service, promotion, and retention beyond the first term) and background characteristics of recruits enlisting in the U.S. Navy between FYs 1978 and 1982. The recruits in the analysis had no prior military service and had initial obligations of four years. Completion of the first term among high school diploma graduates was 71 percent and among certificate-holders was 47 percent (where certificate holders in this study are those with a type of equivalency diploma), a difference of 24 percentage points.

RAND Arroyo Center Analysis

We operationalized potential cost avoidance by increasing the percentage of recruits with a high school diploma from 90 percent to 100 percent, or 7,000 more recruits with a high school diploma for a 70,000 accession mission (70,000 × 0.10). Applying the effect found in the study to these 7,000 recruits resulted in 1,680 potential losses saved. We applied the cost of recruiting and training to potential losses saved to estimate potential annual costs avoided from using education to screen out recruits who have a higher likelihood of not completing their first term. Table 4.7 presents the relevant information.

Table 4.7. Potential Annual Costs Avoided as a Result of Screening on Recruit Education to Reduce First-Term Attrition

Screener	Reduction in Attrition	Number of Accessions Affected	Potential Losses Saved	Recruiting and Training Costs	Potential Annual Costs Avoided
High school graduation	24% [23.24%, 24.76%]	7,000	1,680 [1,627, 1,733]	$75,638	$127.1M [$123.0M, $131.1M]

SOURCES: Study documented in Timothy W. Cooke and Aline O. Quester, "What Characterizes Successful Enlistees in the All-Volunteer Force: A Study of Male Recruits in the U.S. Navy," *Social Science Quarterly*, Vol. 73, No. 2, 1992. Recruiting and training costs derived from ATRRS and HQDA G-1, FY 2018 data.

4.7: First-Term Attrition in the Navy: Causes and Proposed Solutions (Larson and Kewley, 2000)

Description of the Study

This study examines the literature on accession screening procedures for U.S. Navy recruiting as it relates to attrition. Using FY 1995–1998 data on U.S. Navy applicants, the study reports that 98,823 recruits with a high school diploma completed their first year and that 25,963 attrited, an attrition rate of 20.8 percent. Among GED-holders, the one-year attrition rate is 36.1 percent, with 2,885 completing their first year and 1,633 attriting.

RAND Arroyo Center Analysis

We used the attrition rates for high school graduates and GED-holders, as reported in the study, to estimate the potential annual costs avoided from recruiting more high school graduates. Specifically, we applied the difference in the reported attrition rates (36.1 percent – 20.8 percent = 15.3 percentage points) to 7,000 recruits, representing the increase in high school graduates if the Army were to raise the percentage of graduates from 90 percent to 100 percent. We then multiplied the estimated number of potential losses saved by the costs of recruiting and training an IET graduate. As shown in Table 4.8, if the Army recruited 7,000 more high school graduates in lieu of GED holders, the study results suggest that there would be 1,074 fewer first-year losses. At a cost of $75,638 for recruiting and training an IET graduate, this results in potential annual costs avoided of $81,211,040, as shown in Table 4.8.

Table 4.8. Potential Annual Costs Avoided as a Result of Screening on Recruit Education to Reduce One-Year Attrition Rates

Screener	Reduction in Attrition	Number of Accessions Affected	Potential Losses Saved	Recruiting and Training Costs	Potential Annual Costs Avoided
High school graduation	15.3% [14.08%, 16.52%]	7,000	1,074 [989, 1,159]	$75,638	$81.2M [$74.8M, $87.7M]

SOURCES: Gerald E. Larson and Stephanie Booth Kewley, *First-Term Attrition in the Navy: Causes and Proposed Solutions*, Naval Health Research Center, 2000. Recruiting and training costs derived from ATRRS and HQDA G-1, FY 2018 data.

Studies Involving Nonpsychological (Other) Screeners to Reduce First-term Attrition Among Certain MOSs

4.8: Soldier Selection: Past, Present, and Future (Zook, 1996)

Description of the Study

This study was a long-term research program to evaluate and enhance the Army's process of selecting qualified applicants for enlistment and of assigning them to the most appropriate jobs. The study found that it was difficult to improve on the Armed Services Vocational Aptitude Battery (ASVAB), but enhancements to the ASVAB were evaluated. The finding detailed here concerns the portion of the study regarding matching soldiers to jobs, particularly the ASVAB score standards for MOS. The study reports the effect on 36-month attrition rates of raising AFQT cutoff scores to deny enlistment to the lowest 10 percent of scorers previously accepted for a combat MOS (attrition rate reduced by 5 percentage points).

RAND Arroyo Center Analysis

Potential costs avoided were estimated using the percentage point reduction in attrition from raising the cutoff score multiplied by the cost of recruiting and producing an OSUT graduate. The 1,209 potential annual accessions saved estimate was calculated by multiplying the percentage point reduction in attrition by the estimated annual accessions into a combat MOS (24,182).[1] Given the cost of an OSUT graduate for a combat MOS of $60,841 (see Appendix A), we then estimated potential annual costs avoided as $73,561,332. Table 4.9 summarizes the key information.

Table 4.9. Potential Annual Costs Avoided from Using ASVAB Scores in MOS Assignments

Screener	Reduction in Attrition	Annual Combat MOS Accessions	Potential Annual Accessions Saved	Recruiting and Training Costs	Potential Annual Costs Avoided
AFQT score	5% [4.57%, 5.43%]	24,182	1,209 [1,104, 1,314]	$60,841	$73.6M [$67.2M, $79.9M]

SOURCES: Study documented in Lola M. Zook, *Soldier Selection: Past, Present and Future*, Army Research Institute, 19966. Recruiting and training costs derived from HQDA G-1 and ATRRS, FY 2018.

[1] Derived from Regular Army Analyst. Because this finding is only applicable to combat MOS, we used the number of annual accessions in combat MOS only.

Chapter 5. Reenlistment

This chapter presents information on the potential annual costs avoided associated with improving reenlistment and retention through the use of personality tests or other screeners. Table 5.1 categorizes the studies considered in this chapter, providing full titles and assigning study numbers.

Unless otherwise indicated, all effect sizes are in percentage points.

Table 5.1. Reenlistment

Study Number	Name of Study
Studies Involving Personality Tests or Screeners That Could Improve Reenlistment	
5.1	Personality and Success Among Military Enlisted Personnel: An Historical Prospective Study of U.S. Navy Corpsmen (Vickers, Hervig, and Booth, 1996)
5.2	Validating Future Force Performance Measures (Army Class): In-Unit Performance Longitudinal Validation (AIM and RBI) (Knapp, Owens, and Allen, 2012)
Studies Involving the Use of Other Survey-Based Screeners to Improve Reenlistment	
5.3	Validating Future Force Performance Measures (Army Class): In-Unit Performance Longitudinal Validation (WPA Dimensions and WPA Facets) (Knapp, Owens, and Allen, 2012)
5.4	Predicting Retention Rates of U.S. Soldiers Stationed in Europe (Castro and Huffman, 2002)
Studies Involving Nonpsychological (Other) Screeners to Improve Reenlistment	
5.5	What Characterizes Successful Enlistees in the All-Volunteer Force: A Study of Male Recruits in the U.S. Navy (Cooke and Quester, 1992)
5.6	Impact of the Army Continuing Education System (ACES) on Soldier Retention and Performance: Data Analyses (Sticha et al., 2003)
5.7	Effectiveness of the Voluntary Education Program (Garcia, Joy, and Reese, 1998)

Studies Involving Personality Tests or Screeners That Could Improve Reenlistment

5.1: Personality and Success Among Military Enlisted Personnel: An Historical Prospective Study of U.S. Navy Corpsmen (Vickers, Hervig, and Booth, 1996)

Description of the Study

The study examined personality and aptitude predictors of success in male U.S. Navy corpsmen, with success defined as the decision of a corpsmen to reenlist. The study follows first-term enlistees through the term, ending with the decision to reenlist for a second term or not to reenlist. From a pool of 6,303 male sailors who began A School between October 1972 and December 1973, the sample was thinned to select individuals who were most similar in terms of entering status. Using a selection criterion that included first-term enlistees signed to a four-year term as seamen and starting out at a base pay of E-1, the sample was ultimately reduced to 4,512 men.

The study reported that outcomes "included successful completion of A School, a change in occupation after successful completion of A School (pipeline shift), completion of the first-term enlistment, paygrade at the end of the first tour, being recommended for reenlistment, and reenlisting" (Vickers, Hervig, and Booth, 1996). At certain outcomes, including completion of A School and reenlisting, the sample size will have been cut from the previous regression (i.e., the final sample of the reenlistment regression is those who completed A School, completed the first term, and were recommended for reenlistment). Among the measures used to predict outcomes were Comrey Personality Scales, "which include scores for eight general personality domains and for specific personality facets within the domains" (Vickers, Hervig, and Booth, 1996), and mental aptitude, as measured by the ASVAB, specifically, the General Classification Test and the AFQT composite scale scores.

In its prediction model of reenlistment decisions, results were "summarized by point biserial correlations which can be interpreted simply as the difference in probabilities of 'Success' when people above the scale mean are compared to the probability of success for people who score below the mean" (Vickers, Hervig, and Booth, 1996). The study imposed an effect size criterion on the correlations because of the large sample size (2,232 for those with a decision to reenlist, the smallest sample size). Thus, while a correlation of $r = 0.042$ could have been significant in the model, the authors restricted the correlations discussed to $r = 0.10$.

RAND Arroyo Center Analysis

Point biserial correlations for both "Preference for Routine" and "Intolerance for Non-Conformity" (both 0.10) were the measures that were both statistically significant and of sufficient size to be practically significant. As previously, we screened out the lowest 10 percent of scorers on these measures using the shifted mean of the standard normal distribution Z_x (0.195). We also used a recent reenlistment rate of 0.5 (50 percent) and the standard deviation of that rate (also 0.5). The overall percentage point increase in retention was calculated as the correlation between the screening measure and retention times the standard deviation of the reenlistment rate times Z_x, resulting in an estimated increase in the reenlistment rate of 0.975 percentage points.

As discussed in Chapter 2, the SRB needed to achieve the same result was estimated by beginning with the underlying reenlistment rate of 50 percent. Next, the estimated increase in the reenlistment rate (0.975 percentage points) was subtracted from the 50 percent reenlistment rate, yielding 49.025 percent. The magnitude of the proportional reenlistment increase that would be needed to reach 50 percent from 49.025 percent was calculated as 50 / (49.025) – 1= 0.01989. This is then converted to percent (1.989) and used with information from the DRM, as described in Chapter 2.

In this case, the SRB was calculated as $3069.11 = (1.989 / 3.24) × $5000. We then adjusted for inflation, because the DRM table (Table 2.2) reflected 2015 dollars. We inflated by 6.09 percent (Consumer Price Index increase from September 2015 to September 2018), yielding $3,256.02. Last, we multiplied that value by the number of reenlistees (70,000 times 0.6525 reaching the end of their term times 0.5 reenlistment rate = 22,837), to estimate the potential SRB cost avoided. Table 5.2 presents the key results.

Table 5.2. Potential Annual Cost Avoided Due to Increased Reenlistment as a Result of Using Preference for Routine or Intolerance for Nonconformity Scores as a Screener

Screener	Effect Size ($rxSD_y$)	Z_x	Estimated Number of Reenlistees	Estimated SRB Needed	Potential Annual Cost Avoided
Preference for Routine	5% [2.94%, 7.06%]	0.195	22,837	$3,256 [$1,787, $4,372]	$74.4M [$40.8M, $99.9M]
Intolerance for Nonconformity	5% [2.94%, 7.06%]	0.195	22,837	$3,256 [$1,787, $4,372]	$74.4M [$40.8M, $99.9M]

SOURCES: Study documented in Ross R. Vickers, Jr., Linda K. Hervig, and Richard F. Booth, *Personality and Success Among Military Enlisted Personnel: An Historical Prospective Study of U.S. Navy Corpsmen*, Naval Health Research Center, 1996.

5.2: Validating Future Force Performance Measures (Army Class): In-Unit Performance Longitudinal Validation (AIM and RBI) (Knapp, Owens, and Allen, 2012)

Description of the Study

This study identified potential measures for non-cognitive attributes (e.g., interests, values, personality) that the AFQT and education tier do not currently assess. Specifically, this study sought measures that could be used as new predictors to enhance entry-level soldier selection, classification, and retention. This study was conducted by ARI in partnership with the Human Resources Research Organization. Noncognitive assessments and criterion data were collected from approximately 11,000 soldiers across all components (Regular Army, U.S. Army Reserve, U.S. Army National Guard) and across MOS classifications.

This study was a predictive, longitudinal validation effort in which individual difference measures were collected from new soldiers at accession and for retention behaviors (reenlistment intentions) at three career points: end of training, 12 to 24 months in service, and again after 36 months of service. The measures used were Assembling Objects, AIM, TAPAS, predictor Situational Judgement Test, RBI, Army Knowledge Assessment, WPA Dimensions, and WPA Facets. This study used the incremental prediction of each noncognitive measure over education tier to predict first-term reenlistment intentions at 36 months for two units, 1 and 2, operationalized as the change in multiple correlation. We used the final time point of data collection, 36 months, for the following analysis because it was the assessment of retention behavior closest to the actual reenlistment decision. In this write-up, we present the personality test or screener results that were statistically significant for both units. For these measures, ΔR = 0.14 for AIM unit 1; ΔR = 0.13 for AIM unit 2; ΔR = 0.19 for RBI unit 1; and ΔR = 0.20 for RBI unit 2. WPA Dimensions and WPA Facets, the only other two measures that were statistically significant for both units, are covered in the next section.

RAND Arroyo Center Analysis

We estimated potential cost avoidance using the noncognitive measures to screen out the bottom 10 percent of scorers with the lowest likelihood for reenlisting. The percentage point increase in reenlistees was estimated using the reported increments in the multiple correlation times the standard deviation of the reenlistment rate times the new Z_x value. Then, as discussed in Chapter 2, we multiplied this number by 0.37 to reflect the predictive relationship between reenlistment intentions and actual reenlistment (r = 0.37, Campbell and Zook, 1996).

As discussed, the SRB needed to achieve the same result was calculated by subtracting the estimated percentage point increase in the reenlistment rate from 50 percent and then determining the proportional reenlistment increase that would be needed to reach 50 percent from this lower level. Using information from the DRM, we then found the corresponding SRB size using Table 2.2. As before, we inflated by 6.09 percent and multiplied that value by the number of reenlistees to estimate the potential annual SRB cost avoided. Table 5.3 presents the key results for AIM and RBI.

Table 5.3. Potential Annual Cost Avoided Due to Increased Reenlistment as a Result of Using Noncognitive Screeners—AIM, RBI

Screener	Effect Size ($RxSD_y$)	Z_x	Reenlistment Intention r with Reenlistment	Estimated Number of Reenlistees	Estimated SRB Needed	Potential Annual Cost Avoided
AIM unit 1	7% [2.90%, 11.10%]	0.195	0.37	22,837	$1,671 [$648, $2,512]	$38.2M [$14.8M, $57.4M]
AIM unit 2	6.5% [1.76%, 11.24%]	0.195	0.37	22,837	$1,550 [$394, $2,543]	$35.4M [$9.0M, $58.1M]
RBI unit 1	9.5% [6.65%, 12.35%]	0.195	0.37	22,837	$2,276 [$1,496, $2,799]	$52.0M [$34.2M, $63.9M]
RBI unit 2	10% [6.47%, 13.53%]	0.195	0.37	22,837	$2,397 [$1,455, $3,072]	$54.7M [$33.2M, $70.1M]

SOURCE: Study documented in Deidre J. Knapp, Kimberly S. Owens, and Matthew T. Allen, eds., *Validating Future Force Performance Measures (Army Class): In-Unit Performance Longitudinal Validation*, U.S. Army Research Institute for the Behavioral and Social Sciences, 2012.
NOTE: Because each of the noncognitive attributes investigated was reported independently and because no intercorrelations among these measures were reported, each of the predictors was treated separately for the potential cost-avoidance analyses. Thus, it is unknown how these potentially intercorrelated measures may be used in combination in terms of cost avoidance.

Studies Involving the Use of Survey-Based Screeners to Improve Reenlistment

5.3: Validating Future Force Performance Measures (Army Class): In-Unit Performance Longitudinal Validation (WPA Dimensions and WPA Facets) (Knapp, Owens, and Allen, 2012)

Description of the Study

This is the same study described in the previous section. In this write-up, we present the other (nonpersonality) programs and screener results that were statistically significant for both units. For these measures, $\Delta R = 0.15$ for WPA Dimensions for unit 1; $\Delta R = 0.12$ for WPA Dimensions for unit 2; $\Delta R = 0.18$ for WPA Facets for unit 1; and $\Delta R = 0.16$ for WPA Facets for unit 2. AIM and RBI were covered in the previous section.

RAND Arroyo Center Analysis

As before, we estimated potential cost avoidance using the measures to screen out the bottom 10 percent of scorers with the lowest likelihood for reenlisting. The percentage point increase in reenlistees was estimated using the reported increments in the multiple correlation times the standard deviation of the reenlistment rate times the new Z_x value. Then, as discussed in Chapter 2, this number was multiplied by 0.37 to reflect the predictive relationship between reenlistment intentions and actual reenlistment ($r = 0.37$, Campbell and Zook, 1996).

As discussed, the SRB needed to achieve the same result was calculated by subtracting the estimated percentage point increase in the reenlistment rate from 50 percent and then determining the proportional reenlistment increase that would be needed to reach 50 percent from this lower level. Using information from the DRM, we found the corresponding SRB size using Table 2.2. As before, we inflated by 6.09 percent and multiplied that value by the number of reenlistees to estimate the potential annual SRB cost avoided. Table 5.4 presents the key results for WPA Dimensions and WPA Facets.

Table 5.4. Potential Annual Cost Avoided Due to Increased Reenlistment as a Result of Using Noncognitive Screeners—Assembling Objects Test, WPA

Screener	Effect Size ($R \times SD_y$)	Z_x	Reenlistment Intention r with Reenlistment	Estimated Number of Reenlistees	Estimated SRB Needed	Potential Annual Cost Avoided
WPA Dimensions –Unit 1	7.5% [4.82%, 10.18%]	0.195	0.37	22,837	$1,791 [$1,081, $2,301]	$40.9M [$24.7M, $52.5M]
WPA Dimensions –Unit 2	6% [2.71%, 9.29%]	0.195	0.37	22,837	$1,430 [$606, $2,097]	$32.7M [$13.8M, $47.9M]

Screener	Effect Size (R_xSD_y)	Z_x	Reenlistment Intention r with Reenlistment	Estimated Number of Reenlistees	Estimated SRB Needed	Potential Annual Cost Avoided
WPA Facets –Unit 1	9% [6.33%, 11.67%]	0.195	0.37	22,837	$2,154 [$1,423, $2,643]	$49.2M [$32.5M, $60.4M]
WPA Facets –Unit 2	8% [4.73%, 11.27%]	0.195	0.37	22,837	$1,912 [$1,060, $2,552]	$43.7M [$24.2M, $58.3M]

SOURCE: Study documented in Deidre J. Knapp, Kimberly S. Owens, and Matthew T. Allen, eds., *Validating Future Force Performance Measures (Army Class): In-Unit Performance Longitudinal Validation*, U.S. Army Research Institute for the Behavioral and Social Sciences, 2012.
NOTE: Because each of the noncognitive attributes investigated was reported independently and because no intercorrelations among these measures were reported, each of the predictors was treated separately for the potential cost-avoidance analyses. Thus, it is unknown how these potentially intercorrelated measures may be used in combination in terms of cost avoidance.

5.4: Predicting Retention Rates of U.S. Soldiers Stationed in Europe (Castro and Huffman, 2002)

Description of the Study

This study evaluated whether the commonly cited concerns over the high pace of military operations (operational tempo [OPTEMPO]) and poor work climate negatively affect reenlistment intentions. OPTEMPO was operationalized as a composite of the average hours worked per day, days worked per week, days spent training, and days on temporary duty. Work climate was measured using self-reported job satisfaction, job recognition, task significance, work intensity, job challenge, goal acceptance, job control, and soldier pride.

To assess the effect of OPTEMPO and work climate, the relationship between these two composites and their interaction were used to predict reenlistment intentions using a multinomial logistic regression model. This study reported an overall effect size (pseudo $r = 0.80$) between OPTEMPO and work climate with first-term reenlistment intention rates based on this logistic regression model.

RAND Arroyo Center Analysis

We estimated potential annual costs avoided using the estimated percentage point increase in the reenlistment rate attributable to improving OPTEMPO and work climate by 10 percent. The pseudo *r* was multiplied by the square root of the reenlistment rate (0.5) to give the effect size. This was next transformed into the percentage point increase in first-term reenlistments by multiplying first by Z_x and then by 37 percent to reflect the predictive relationship between reenlistment intentions and actual reenlistment ($r = 0.37$, Campbell and Zook, 1996). As discussed earlier, the SRB needed to achieve the same result was estimated by subtracting the estimated percentage point increase in the reenlistment rate from 50 percent and calculating the proportional reenlistment increase that would be needed to reach 50 percent from this lower level. We again used the DRM table to interpolate the required SRB value. Once the bonus was estimated, we adjusted for inflation, then multiplied that value by the number of reenlistees to estimate the potential annual SRB cost avoided.

Table 5.5 presents the key results. The cost of improving OPTEMPO and work climate to generate the potential annual savings is unknown. However, because OPTEMPO was operationalized as a composite of the average hours worked per day, days worked per week, days spent training, and days on temporary duty, we believe that the cost of providing the reduction in work time is likely less than the potential cost avoided of nearly $225 million dollars per year.

Table 5.5. Potential Annual Cost Avoided Due to Increased Reenlistment as a Result of Improving OPTEMPO and Work Climate

Screener	Effect Size ($r \times SD_y$)	Z_x	Reenlistment Intention *r* with Reenlistment	Estimated Number of Reenlistees	Estimated SRB Needed	Potential Annual Cost Avoided
Improving OPTEMPO and work climate by 10%	40% [36.53%, 43.47%]	0.195	0.37	22,837	$9,846 [$8,493, $10,133]	$224.9M [$194.0M, $231.4M]

SOURCE: Study documented in Carl Andrew Castro and Ann H. Huffman, *Predicting Retention Rates of U.S. Soldiers Stationed in Europe*, Army Medical Research Unit–Europe, 2002.

Studies Involving Nonpsychological (Other) Screeners to Improve Reenlistment

5.5: What Characterizes Successful Enlistees in the All-Volunteer Force: A Study of Male Recruits in the U.S. Navy (Cooke and Quester, 1992)

Description of the Study

This study explores the relationship between career outcomes (e.g., completion of obligated service, promotion, and retention beyond the first term) and background characteristics of recruits enlisting in the U.S. Navy between FYs 1978 and 1982. The recruits in the analysis had no prior military service and had an initial obligation of four years. In a logistic regression with a dependent variable indicating whether the service member was retained beyond the initial obligation, the coefficient on diploma graduate, AFQT score I–IIIA was 0.036. The coefficient on certificate (a type of equivalency diploma) was –0.579.

RAND Arroyo Center Analysis

Using the coefficients and the distribution of the study population, we estimated the reenlistment rate when 90 percent of the enlistees were high school graduates and 10 percent were certificate holders and when 100 percent were graduates and took the difference in the two rates, which was equal to 1.4573 percent.

The size of the SRB needed to achieve the increase in reenlistments equivalent to that estimated in the study was calculated using information from the DRM, as described earlier. As also described earlier, the potential annual costs avoided are those that would be needed using SRBs to provide the same increases in reenlistments as the increases estimated for a high school diploma rate of 100 percent versus 90 percent. In this instance for regression-based results, the percentage increase for reenlistments needed is calculated against the lower 36 percent reported in the study. So, the percentage is estimated as $[0.36 / (0.36 - 0.014573) - 1] \times 100$, which equals 4.218836 percent. Using the SRB methodology described in Chapter 2, we calculated a bonus of $6,452.28, which we inflated to $6845.223 and applied to the total number of recent reenlistees. As Table 5.6 shows, the study suggests that recruiting 100 percent high school graduates rather than 90 percent results in potential annual SRB costs avoided of $156.3 million.

Table 5.6. Potential Annual Cost Avoided as a Result of Increased Retention from Screening in More High School Graduates

Screener	Increase in Reenlistment	Estimated Number of Reenlistees	Estimated SRB Needed	Potential Annual Cost Avoided
High school graduation	1.46% [1.34%, 1.58%]	22,837	$6,845 [$6,277, $7,417]	$156.3M [$143.4M, $169.4M]

SOURCE: Study documented in Timothy W. Cooke and Aline O. Quester, "What Characterizes Successful Enlistees in the All-Volunteer Force: A Study of Male Recruits in the U.S. Navy," *Social Science Quarterly*, Vol. 73, No. 2, 1992.

5.6: Impact of the Army Continuing Education System (ACES) on Soldier Retention and Performance: Data Analyses (Sticha et al., 2003)

Description of the Study

This study evaluated whether the ACES Tuition Assistance (TA) and Functional Academic Skills Training (FAST) programs improved first-term reenlistment. Sticha et al., 2003, investigated the impact of TA and FAST on first-term soldiers' reenlistment decisions. However, not all individuals participate in TA and FAST, and some of the same individual differences that lead soldiers to take advantage of these programs also are independently correlated with reenlistment decisions. Thus, this study used a bivariate probit regression to estimate a percentage point increase in first-term reenlistment rates attributable to TA participation after controlling for these other influences (see p. 38 of the study). That is, this model estimates the joint probability that an individual will participate in tuition assistance and then reenlist, after controlling for opportunities to participate, demographics (race and gender), and AFQT score (continuous) (see p. 37). As reported, TA and FAST show the potential to increase reenlistment by 7.6 and 1.4 percentage points, respectively (see p. 37).[1] The study reported that 28 percent and 21 percent of soldiers participated in TA and FAST, respectively (see p. 32).

RAND Arroyo Center Analysis

Our analysis used the percentage point increase in the reenlistment rate attributable to TA or FAST participation reported in this study times the reported proportion of soldiers participating in TA or FAST to estimate the potential overall percentage point increase in reenlistments due to TA and FAST. As discussed earlier, the SRB needed to achieve the same result was estimated beginning with the reported reenlistment rate of 35 percent and subtracting the estimated percentage point increase in the reenlistment rate. The proportional reenlistment increase that would be needed to reach 35 percent from this lower level was then calculated and converted to a percentage increase. We then used the DRM table to interpolate the required SRB value. Once the bonus was estimated, we adjusted for inflation, then multiplied that value by the number of reenlistees in Table 5.7 to estimate the potential annual SRB cost avoided. As shown in Table 5.7, the study suggests that TA results in a potential annual SRB cost avoidance of $223,748,203 and that FAST results in a potential annual SRB cost avoidance of $29,854,295. We were unable to document the cost of providing these programs.

Table 5.7. Potential Annual Cost Avoided Due to Increased Reenlistment as a Result of Participation in Tuition Assistance or Functional Academic Skills Training

ACES Intervention	Increase in Reenlistment	Proportion of Usage	Estimated Number of Reenlistees	Estimated SRB Needed	Potential Annual Cost Avoided
TA	7.6% [1.82%, 13.38%]	28%	22,837	$9,798 [$2,276, $17,744]	$223.7M [$52.0M, $405.2M]
FAST	1.4% [0.33%, 2.47%]	21%	22,837	$1,307 [$311, $2,317]	$29.9M [$7.1M; $52.9M]

SOURCE: Study documented in Paul J. Sticha, Timothy A. Dall, Kristina Handy, Javier Espinosa, Paul. F. Hogan, and Mark C. Young, *Impact of the Army Continuing Education System (ACES) on Soldier Retention and Performance: Data Analyses*, U.S. Army Research Institute for the Behavioral and Social Sciences, 2003.

[1] In contrast to TA, participation in FAST should be considered an *upper* bound estimate of the true effect because, unlike TA, the bivariate probit model did not simultaneously control for the possible bias of self-selection among individuals who choose to participate in the FAST program. FAST participation was similarly correlated with soldier characteristics, e.g., lower AFQT category and race, both of which are known to be correlated with retention and reenlistment. However, the model controlled for these characteristics; this likely helped to reduce possible omitted variable bias.

5.7: Effectiveness of the Voluntary Education Program (Garcia, Joy, and Reese, 1998)

Description of the Study

The study provided an analysis of the Navy's Voluntary Education (VOLED) program's effects on retention. The program includes TA, the Program for Afloat College Education, and the Academic Skills Learning Centers.

The VOLED "program provides off-duty educational opportunities integrating a variety of continuing education programs to sailors seeking to enhance their professional and personal growth" (Garcia, Joy, and Reese, 1998). VOLED helps sailors pursue a college degree through such programs as tuition assistance. According to Garcia, Joy, and Reese, sailors with more college credits are more likely to reenlist. In FY 1997, 61,000 enlistees participated, with an additional 4,700 coming from officers and Marines, and with a majority (77 percent) of participants using TA as their primary source of help. The data used included 600,000 enlisted sailors between 1992 and 1997. Credits, including college level, academic skills level, and developmental level, were observed in the TA and the Program for Afloat College Education. At the time of this study, most Academic Skills Learning Centers had only been in operation for a few months; thus, no data were collected from these sites.

The study used a binomial probit model to study the effect of VOLED on retention, where the predicted variable was reenlistment or extension. There is a concern about potential sample bias in the study because sailors who are more likely to reenlist may also be more likely to take advantage of VOLED. To adjust for this, the study model first predicted what type of sailor may have a predisposition to participate in VOLED, then predicted retention using expected participation as a control.

The study reported the estimated marginal effects of different measures on reenlistment. Within VOLED, the number of college credits, participation in the Academic Skills program, and developmental credits were significant in increasing retention. Other measures were statistically controlled for, including education at accession, qualification for an SRB, pay grade at decision point, percentage of time at sea, demographics (gender and race), dependents, whether a spouse is also in the military, the unemployment rate, and different dummies for various occupations.

RAND Arroyo Center Analysis

We used only the marginal effects from the individual programs that were reported to be statistically significant; this included College Credits (0.42 percentage point), Academic Skills participation (35.17 percentage points), and developmental credits (1.94 percentage points). We used our best estimate for the proportion of usage, which is the percentage of enlistees who use Academic Skill Training. Our analysis used the reported increase in the reenlistment rate times the proportion of soldiers participating to estimate the potential overall percentage point increase in reenlistments.

As discussed earlier, the SRBs that would be needed to achieve the same results as the increases estimated for College Credits, Academic Skills Participation, and Developmental Credits were estimated beginning with reenlistment rates of 31, 34, and 34 percent, respectively, as reported in the study, then subtracting the estimated percentage point increase reenlistments, and then calculating the proportional reenlistment increase that would be needed to reach the reported reenlistment from this lower level. We then used the DRM table to interpolate the required SRB value and adjusted for inflation. Last, we multiplied that value by the number of reenlistees in Table 5.8 to estimate the potential annual SRB cost avoided.

Table 5.8 presents the key results. We were unable to estimate the cost of providing the VOLED programs.

Table 5.8. Potential Annual Cost Avoided Due to Increased Reenlistment as a Result of Participation in VOLED

Program	Increase in Reenlistment	Proportion of Usage	Estimated Number of Reenlistees	Estimated SRB Needed	Potential Annual Cost Avoided
College Credits	0.42% [0.17%, 0.69%]	21%	22,837	$440 [$179, $723]	$10.1M [$4.1M, $16.5M]
Academic Skills Participation	35.17% [8.03%, 62.31%]	21%	22,837	$40,404 [$8,054, $108,734]	$922.7M [$183.9M, $2.4B]
Developmental Credits	1.94% [0.19%, 4.31%]	21%	22,837	$1,872 [$181, $4,221]	$42.7M [$4.1M, $96.4M]

SOURCE: Study documented in Federico E. Garcia, Ernest H. Joy, and David L. Reese, *Effectiveness of the Voluntary Education Program*, Center for Naval Analyses, 1998.

Chapter 6. Other Non-Health Outcomes

This chapter presents information on the potential annual costs avoided associated with a variety of other outcomes not already discussed, and not including health (which will be presented in Chapter 7). Table 6.1 categorizes the studies considered in this chapter, providing full titles and assigning study numbers.

Table 6.1. Other Non-Health Studies

Study Number	Name of Study
Studies Involving Approaches to Increasing Recruiter Productivity	
6.1	Evaluation and Refinement of a Screening Instrument for U.S. Army Recruiters: Noncommissioned Officer Leadership Skills Inventory (Horgen et al., 2006)
Studies of Time Saving Resulting from the Use of Computer-Based Training	
6.2	Navy Self-Paced Computer-Based Courses: Practical Implications of Saving Time Under Instruction (UI) (Carey, Reese, and Shuford, 2010)
6.3	Online Training: An Evaluation of the Effectiveness and Efficiency of Training Law Enforcement Personnel over the Internet (Schmeeckle, 2003)
Studies Involving Optimization of Recruiting Resources	
6.4	Resources Required to Meet Army's Enlisted Recruiting Requirements Under Alternative Recruiting Goals, Conditions, and Eligibility Policies (Knapp et al., 2018)
Studies Estimating Costs Associated with Alternative Recruit Selection Policies	
6.5	Prospective Outcome Assessment for Alternative Recruit Selection Policies (Orvis et al., 2018)
6.6	Cost-Effectiveness Analysis of the U.S. Army Assessment of Recruit Motivation and Strength (ARMS) Program (Niebuhr et al., 2013)
Studies Involving the Use of Health Screenings to Reduce Alcohol Misuse and Alcohol-Related Behaviors	
6.7	Screening for Alcohol Misuse and Alcohol-Related Behaviors Among Combat Veterans (Santiago et al., 2010)

Studies Involving Approaches to Increasing Recruiter Productivity

6.1: Evaluation and Refinement of a Screening Instrument for U.S. Army Recruiters: Noncommissioned Officer Leadership Skills Inventory (Horgen et al., 2006)

Description of the Study

The authors indicate that the "NLSI [Noncommissioned Officer Leadership Skills Inventory] measures skills and abilities related to NCO performance, including work orientation, interpersonal skills, and leadership capability." The study was conducted to quantify the association between NLSI scores and Army recruiter performance. This included training attrition and recruiters' enlisted contract production. The NLSI score was found to be associated with recruiter productivity. The bottom 5 percent of NLSI scorers wrote 1.02 contracts per month, whereas the top 5 percent of scorers wrote 1.21 contracts per month. The overall average was 1.09 contracts per month.

RAND Arroyo Center Analysis

We estimated the increase in recruiter productivity that could be achieved by eliminating recruiter candidates scoring in the bottom 5 percent on the NLSI and replacing them with candidates scoring in the upper 95 percent. This was done by estimating the resulting change in the average rate of 1.09 contracts per recruiter each month, as follows. We first derived the rate for the middle 90 percent of NLSI scorers. We then replaced the bottom 5 percent of scorers on NLSI with candidates scoring in upper 95 percent, using both the derived rate and the rate assessed for recruiters scoring in the top 5 percent on the NLSI. The proportions of recruiters in the middle 90 percent and the upper 5 percent were adjusted to 90/95 and 5/95 to account for 100 percent of the recruiters. This resulted in a change in contract production to an average of 1.093684 contracts per recruiter per month. The number of on-production Regular Army recruiters at our study point (7,650 at the end of FY 2018, according to the Army's recruiter data file) was then reduced to the estimated number needed given the improvement in productivity ($7{,}650 \times 1.09 / 1.093684 = 7{,}624$ recruiters). We estimated potential cost avoidance using the estimated savings in the number of recruiters needed given the improvement in productivity. The savings of 26 recruiters was multiplied by $118,000 per recruiter (Army-provided estimate). Table 6.2 presents the results.

Table 6.2. Potential Annual Cost Avoided Due to Increased Recruiter Productivity Using the NLSI

Recruiter Selection	Improvement in Contracts per Month per Recruiter	Baseline Contracts per Month per Recruiter	Recruiters	Potential Recruiters Saved	Cost per Recruiter	Potential Annual Cost Avoided
Replace bottom 5% NLSI scorers with upper 95% scorers	3.68×10^{-3}	1.09	7,650	26	$118,000	$3.0M

SOURCE: Study documented in Kristen E. Horgen, U. Christean Kubisiak, Valentina Bruk-Lee, Patrick W. Connell, Lisa M. Penney, Walter C. Borman, Victoria L. Pace, Elizabeth Lentz, Leonard A. White, Mark C. Young, and Stephen V. Bowles, *Evaluation and Refinement of a Screening Instrument for U.S. Army Recruiters: Noncommissioned Officer Leadership Skills Inventory*, U.S. Army Research Institute for the Behavioral and Social Sciences, March 2006.
NOTES: The study included no standard error information or other results that could be used to generate confidence intervals. The number of recruiters comes from the Army's recruiter data file.

Studies of Cost Savings Resulting from the Use of Computer-Based Training

6.2: Navy Self-Paced Computer-Based Courses: Practical Implications of Saving Time Under Instruction (UI) (Carey, Reese, and Shuford, 2010)

Description of the Study

The objective of this study was to determine course length reductions in Navy A School and Apprentice Technical Training courses (taken during IET) through conversion of traditional training to self-paced CBT. After the conversion, the cost per training hour stayed relatively constant because training was still completed in residence, with a full complement of training staff who became more mentors than instructors. The goal in making the conversions was to decrease the average time students spent in training before being assigned to units. This study took a detailed look at three of the Navy A School course conversions.

Converting courses to a computerized self-paced format decreased the average time to complete courses by 12–42 percent (see Table 6.3).

Table 6.3. Summary of Hours Spent on Group-Paced and Self-Paced Formats

Course	Group-Paced Hours	Self-Paced Hours	Percent Reduction Under CBT
Electronics Technician	140.7	110.2	21.7%
Fire Controlman	80.3	70.8	11.8%
Yeoman	43.8	25.2	42.5%

RAND Arroyo Center Analysis

We estimated the potential Army training cost avoided from reducing AIT course length, net of the cost of CBT conversion and maintenance. We applied the Navy experience to ten Army AIT courses in FY 2014 and calculated the potential cost avoided from the reduction in course hours. As discussed in Chapter 2, the calculations required: (1) choice of which Army courses to convert to CBT, (2) determination of the number of course hours reduced, (3) calculation of the cost of converting course hours to CBT, and (4) determination of the cost of training per course hour. Each step is addressed in the following subsections.

Courses to Convert

We chose AIT courses of types similar to those converted in the Navy (i.e., electronics, administrative, and supply-related courses) and that had sufficient throughput to justify conversion (generally, at least 500 enrollees in ATRRS per year). This resulted in the list of ten courses in Table 6.4. Approximately 128 weeks of training were involved in total and, assuming 40 hours of training per week, 5,112 total training hours.

Table 6.4. Army AIT Courses Used to Estimate Potential Savings from Conversion to Computer-Based Format

MOS	Course Name	2014 Enrollments	Length of Course (in Weeks)
42A	Human Resources Specialist	2,831	9.0
27D	Paralegal Specialist	557	10.6
25N	Nodal Network Systems Operator-Maintainer	669	25.2
25Q	Multichannel Trans System Operator-Maintainer	937	15.0
25U	Signal Support Systems Specialist	1,687	16.0
91C	Utilities Equipment Repairer	744	13.0
91D	Power Generation Equipment Repairer	1,010	10.6
92A	Automated Logistical Specialist	2,231	9.4
92Y	Unit Supply Specialist	2,318	8.4
92F	Petroleum Supply Specialist	2,821	10.6

Calculation of the Reduction in Training Hours

We assumed that AIT course lengths could be reduced by 12 percent on average. This is the low end of the reduction determined in the Navy courses in the study. We chose a conservative estimate because a follow-up analysis by the Navy Inspector General implied that the designers may have gone too far in training hour cuts in the Navy case. The 12-percent figure is also consistent with the research findings that 40 percent of the course hours of a typical course could be converted and that, on average, the reduction in learning time for a course hour converted was 30 percent (Shanley et al., 2012, p. 20). Using this information, 2,045 hours were converted to CBT (40 percent of 5,112), and course hours were reduced by 613 (12 percent of 5,112). Given the range in enrollments from 557 to 2,831 in the ten courses, we weighted the respective course length reductions by the corresponding course enrollments to estimate that an average of 1,408 enrollees per course hour were saved.

Calculation of Cost to Convert

As discussed in Chapter 2, each course hour converted requires an initial investment and yearly maintenance. The cost per hour to convert learning to CBT has been estimated at $28,588 (Shanley et al., 2012, updated for inflation). We assumed the conversion would need to be redone every six years and that the annual maintenance cost per year would be 25 percent of the total cost (Granja-Alvarez and Barranco-García, 1997). Thus, we estimated that the annualized cost per course hour to convert training to CBT was $11,912 ($28,588, plus 0.25 of $28,588 times 6, all divided by 6).

Determination of Training Cost

As also discussed in Chapter 2, the cost of a training hour was derived from TRADOC's ATRM-159 analysis for AIT courses. As noted there, in 2014, the average cost of an AIT graduate was $30,700 for a 12-week course. We adjusted the first figure to $29,238 as the cost per enrollee (assuming a 5 percent attrition rate for this course-from ATRRS 2014) and 40 hours of instruction weekly. Thus, we estimated that the cost of AIT training per enrollee per course hour was $29,238 / (12 × 40) = $61.

Potential Cost Avoided

We then calculated the overall potential training cost avoided as $52,649,344 and subtracted the $24,360,040 cost of course conversion and maintenance, for a net potential cost avoidance of $28,289,304, and adjusted it to 2018 dollars. Table 6.5 summarizes the key information.

Table 6.5. Potential Annual Cost Avoided from Reducing AIT Course Length Through the Use of Computer-Based Training

	1. Reduction in Course Length (%)	2. Course Hours in 10 Courses	3. Reduction in Course Hours (1 × 2)	4. Average Throughput per Course Hour Saved	5. AIT Training Cost per Hour per Enrollee	6. Training Cost Avoided (3 × 4 × 5)	7. % Hours Converted to CBT	8. Hours Converted (7 × 2)	9. Annual Cost per Hour Converted	10. Annual Cost of Conversion (9 × 8)	Potential Annual Cost Avoided from Conversion (6 – 10) ($2018)
CBT	12.00%	5,112	613	1,408	$61	$52,649,344	40.00%	2,045	$11,912	$24,360,040	$30.0M

SOURCES: Study documented in Neil Carey, David Reese, and Robert Shuford, “Navy Self-Paced Computer-Based Courses: Practical Implications of Saving Time Under Instruction (UI),” *Military Psychology*, Vol. 22, No. 4, 2010. Also, Naval Inspector General, *Report to the Secretary of the Navy, Computer Based Training*, March 2009.

Cost and time implications of CBT conversion from Shanley et al., 1997.

NOTES: Actual results on computer-based training. Confidence intervals not applicable. Throughput in ten AIT courses during 2014 from ATRRS. Courses are Human Resource Specialist (42A), Paralegal Specialist (27D), Nodal Network Systems Operator-Maintainer (25N), Multichannel Transmission System Operator-Maintainer (25Q), Signal Support Systems Specialist (25U), Utilities Equipment Repairer (91C), Power Generation Equipment Repairer (91D), Automated Logistical Specialist (92A), Unit Supply Specialist (92Y), and Petroleum Supply Specialist (92F). Cost of AIT courses estimated from ATRRS data and from TRADOC’s ATRM-159 analysis for AIT courses.

6.3: Online Training: An Evaluation of the Effectiveness and Efficiency of Training Law Enforcement Personnel over the Internet (Schmeeckle, 2003)

Description of the Study

This study compared the cost effectiveness of Computer Assisted Instruction (CAI) with that of classroom instruction in a jail management course at the Nebraska Law Enforcement Training Center in 1999. Cost effectiveness included both the effectiveness of the learning and the cost of the training. The 101 trainees who participated were randomly assigned to online and classroom training. (They averaged nearly 33 years of age, and one-half were men.) Among the lessons converted to online training were transporting inmates, hostage survival, jail disturbances, and jail suicides. CAI decreased the average time to complete the course by 50 percent using the same instructional staff. A cost-benefit analysis showed substantial cost avoidance for the course.

RAND Arroyo Center Analysis

As true for Study 6.2, we estimated potential training cost avoidance for appropriate course(s) in the Army from reducing course length, net of the cost of CAI conversion and maintenance. In this case, we applied the Nebraska Law Enforcement Training Center experience to the Army's MP OSUT course in 2014, calculating the cost avoided from the reduction of course hours. MP OSUT training is 760 hours in total and has substantial field components not suitable for CAI conversion. Therefore, we were conservative in estimating the number of training hours that could be converted. More specifically, we assumed the same number of hours would be converted in the MP course as had been converted in the Nebraska course (40 hours), resulting in a 50-percent reduction in the hours of instruction (i.e., 20 hours reduction). As discussed earlier, the cost per hour to convert learning to CAI was estimated at $28,588, and the annualized cost per course hour to convert training to CAI was estimated to be $11,912.

The cost of a training hour in the MP course was derived from information from MPA, plus ATRRS information for MP OSUT in 2014. Because MP OSUT was a longer-than-average OSUT course, we proportionally increased the MPA estimated cost to $40,064. We then adjusted that figure downward to $33,021 as the cost per enrollee (based on a 17.6 percent attrition rate from ATRRS 2014) and assumed that each week involved 40 hours of instruction. Thus, we estimated that the cost of AIT training per enrollee per course hour was $33,021 / (19.2 weeks × 40 hours/week) = $43.

We then calculated the overall potential training cost avoided as $3,025,480 and subtracted the $476,480 cost of course conversion and maintenance, for a net potential annual cost avoidance of $2,549,000, and adjusted that to 2018 dollars. Table 6.6 summarizes the key information.

Table 6.6. Potential Annual Cost Avoided from Reducing Army Law Enforcement Course Lengths Through the Use of Computer Assisted Instruction

	1. % Reduction in Training Hours	2. Hours Converted	3. Reduction in Training Hours (1 × 2)	4. FY 2014 Throughput-MP OSUT	5. OSUT Training Cost per Hour per Enrollee	6. Training Cost Saved (3 × 4 × 5)	7. Annual Cost per Hour Converted	8. Annual Cost of Conversion (2 × 6)	Potential Annual Cost Avoided from Conversion (6 – 8) (in $2018)
CAI	50.00%	40	20	3,518	$43	$3,025,480	$11,912	$476,480	$2.9M

SOURCES: Study documented in Joyce M. Schmeeckle, "Online Training: An Evaluation of the Effectiveness and Efficiency of Training Law Enforcement Personnel Over the Internet," *Journal of Science Education and Technology*, Vol. 12, No. 3, September 2003. Cost of CAI conversion from Shanley et al., 2012. Cost of CBT maintenance from Granja-Alvarez and Barranco-García, 1997. Cost of MP OSUT course estimated from ATRRS data (to get length and graduation rate information) and average training cost information from HQDA G-1, converted to a cost per MP OSUT course hour.
NOTES: Actual results on CBT. Confidence intervals not applicable.

Studies Involving Optimization of Recruiting Resources

6.4: Resources Required to Meet Army's Enlisted Recruiting Requirements Under Alternative Recruiting Goals, Conditions, and Eligibility Policies (Knapp et al., 2018)

Description of the Study

The purpose of the study was to integrate results of past research and conduct new analyses on alternative recruiting resource levels and mix and enlistment eligibility policies to develop the RRM and tool, examine trade-offs in resource and recruit-characteristic policies to achieve varying Army active enlisted recruiting goals under varying recruiting conditions, and use the model and tool to identify cost-minimizing portfolios of resources and policies to address specific recruiting requirements, conditions, and time horizons.

The study examined development of the RRM, enlistment effects of changes in the levels and mix of recruiting resources, and results from application of the model to alternative recruiting requirements, unemployment rates, enlistment eligibility conditions, and timelines.[1] The report also compares costs for RRM-based optimal recruiting strategies (recruiting resource levels and

---

[1] Data used in the RRM came from a number of sources broadly falling into three categories: military data, advertising data, and economic or demographic data. The military data used were drawn primarily from databases that the Army's Human Resources Command and Recruiting Command (USAREC) maintains. Overall recruiting missions are issued by HQDA G-1. Recruiter data on status and location come from USAREC and track each recruiter's current monthly status and assignment. The data used cover August 2002 through September 2015. USAREC collected data on monthly contract missions and achievements down to the station level. Data on contracts written and accessions into the Army are drawn from the Regular Army Analyst file. The detailed enlistee data used captures all enlistees from FY 2001 forward.

The model relies on economic and demographic data measured consistently in the 50 states and the District of Columbia. Data concerning the training seats planned for future months were drawn from the accession mission letters issued by HQDA G-1. Television advertising data used in the analysis matches actual payments with the dates that commercials were aired and the resulting marketing impressions. The Army Marketing and Research Group and the Army's advertising agency provided highly detailed commercial cost and impression data for FYs 2012–2015, the longest period for which such detailed data have been collected.

The analysis focuses on the resources expended in a recruiting company area during a month and prior months. The analysis uses TV prospect (versus influencer or general population) advertising spending and prospect impressions, because this type of advertising has the most direct theoretical effect on enlistment contract production. Because recruiting success varies with economic and population size differences across areas, the model used economic and demographic factors. They were based on Woods and Poole projections of qualified military available youth. As the study reports, "Qualified military available youth are defined as U.S. citizens 17–24 years of age who are eligible and available for enlisted military service without a waiver. Ineligibility is based on (1) medical/physical, (2) overweight, (3) mental health, (4) drugs, (5) conduct, (6) dependents, and (7) aptitude criteria." Unemployment rates were based on the Current Population Survey (administered monthly to households by the U.S. Census Bureau) and computed by the U.S. Bureau of Labor Statistics.

In general, data were collected so that they would correspond to the recruiting resources, enlistment eligibility policies, and economic conditions in effect as of each calendar month from August 2002 through September 2015.

The modeling method in the study used a number of different specifications that accounted for lagged effects of key measures of broad economic and Army-specific data.

mix, enlistment eligibility policies) with those for an incentive-centric strategy focusing heavily on enlistment bonuses.

RAND Arroyo Center Analysis

The study used 16 years of data on enlistments, resources, and eligibility policies to carry out the underlying analyses required to develop the RRM. The RRM is used to examine trade-offs in resource and recruit-characteristic policies to achieve Army active enlisted recruiting goals under specific recruiting requirements and conditions and to identify a cost-minimizing mix of resources and policies to address the needs and conditions.

We compared the optimized cost with the cost of an incentive-centric approach to meet the same 75,000 accession requirement,[2] holding eligibility constant. To calculate the difference in cost between the RRM optimal recruiting resource levels and mix and an incentive-centric strategy, we used the RRM to identify a cost-minimizing mix of resources and policies to address the recruiting requirements and conditions noted below Table 6.7. This is repeated for the incentive-centric approach, a strategy that first relies on increased bonuses to meet the requirements, then optimally supplements the bonuses with the other recruiting resources, as needed.

Table 6.7. Potential Annual Costs Avoided from Using Optimal Recruiting Resource Levels Versus Incentive-Centric Strategy

Accession Goal	Unemployment Rate	Recruiter Cost Avoided ($M)	TV Advertising Cost Avoided ($M)	Bonus Cost Avoided ($M)	Potential Annual Total Cost Avoided
75,000	4.80%	(27)	(37)	419	$354M

SOURCES: Study documented in David Knapp, Bruce R. Orvis, Christopher Maerzluft, and Tiffany Berglund, *Resources Required to Meet Army's Enlisted Recruiting Requirements Under Alternative Recruiting Goals, Conditions, and Eligibility Policies*, RAND Corporation, RR-2364-A, 2018.
NOTES: Simulation results. Study methodology does not support generation of confidence intervals. The RRM optimizes monthly resource obligations to achieve an accession goal of 75,000 and an end-of-year Delayed Entry Program (DEP) goal of 20,000. Key assumptions include monthly training seats based on original FY 2017 HQDA G-1 mission letter distribution; 8,800 recruiters at FY start; $8 million, $5.7 million, $8.7 million, $7.1 million, $0.2 million, and $0.2 million in monthly advertising spending prior to FY start (April–September, respectively); 12,500 entry DEP; the recruiting environment reflects economic conditions remaining constant, with unemployment at 4.8 percent. In the incentive-centric scenario, bonuses are used first to accomplish FY objectives and, if there is an accession shortfall, the RRM uses other resources to make up the difference.

[2] We had to use 75,000 accessions in this case because the results reported were based on that number and because the change in cost related to changes in the number of accessions is not linear.

Studies Estimating Costs Associated with Alternative Recruit Selection Policies

6.5: Prospective Outcome Assessment for Alternative Recruit Selection Policies (Orvis et al., 2018)

Description of the Study

The purpose of the study was to identify the prospective effects of combinations of new recruits' cognitive, noncognitive, physical, demographic, and behavioral attributes on serving successfully and completing the first term and on related costs.

The study examined the association of various enlistment characteristics identified in a literature review and in exploratory analyses with DEP, training, and first-term attrition; with adverse intermediate factors, such as a bar to reenlistment or demotion; and with the reason for losses. The independent and joint effects of the characteristics are considered. The recruiting, training, and replacement costs associated with alternative combinations of enlistment characteristics were assessed.

The study used 11 years of enlistment data from the Regular Army Analyst database, allowing at least a four-and-one-half year follow-up of recruits through March 2016 using the TAPDB and Army Training Requirements and Resources System data. The research tool quantifies the results of changes in specific recruit characteristics on the noted outcomes using a set of characteristic weights for each recruit. The weights are all initialized to a value of 1.0. The user chooses the desired levels of the recruit characteristics he or she wishes to change. The weighted results are then used to determine the new outcome levels.

RAND Arroyo Center Analysis

Based on the estimated starting and ending values for the noted outcomes, the study then calculated a total cost for the baseline recruit eligibility levels and the excursion levels. As described in Orvis et al., 2018, pp. 78–79:

> This calculation requires adjusting for changes in average months served, because such changes require adjusting the accession goal in order to maintain first-term strength. The adjustment uses the number of months served on average in the baseline case and divides that by the average months served in the contract period calculated for the excursion. This ratio is then multiplied by the baseline accession goal. The revised accession goal is multiplied by the average cost of training an individual in the excursion. The cost accounts for differences in training success associated with the scenario's changes in recruit characteristics. While the same calculation can be applied to the average recruiting cost, we can do better by taking advantage of the RRM in lieu of using the tool's direct calculation for the scenario.

We explored two changes to expand supply. The first increased the percentage of Tier 2 recruits from 5 percent to 10 percent. The second increased nontraffic, nonfelony offense waivers from 0 percent to 10 percent instead. The unemployment rate was assumed to be 4 percent. The baseline assumes 5 percent Tier 2, 0 percent non–traffic offense waivers, and 3,000 prior-service recruits.

The results in Table 6.8 are based on changes in attrition rates and timing, training performance and related costs, and changes in required recruiting resources due to changes in the accession requirement and recruit characteristics. The results show that both changes lower the average man-months served during the term of enlistment. The changes are of limited size, however: –0.25 months for the Tier 2 increase and only –0.10 months for the waiver increase. The increased loss rate raises the accession requirement to maintain first-term strength, as the table shows. The increased number of accessions required raises training cost. Despite the increase in the number of accessions needed due to the reduction in average man-months served, however, recruiting costs decline substantially due to the effects of increasing the supply of eligible potential enlistees (and the lower cost of Tier 2 recruits). The estimated potential annual costs avoided for a 70,000-accession requirement range from $188 million to $296 million, depending on the eligibility change. Table 6.8 summarizes the results.

Table 6.8. Potential Annual Cost Avoided Due to Increasing Tier 2 Recruits or Increasing Nontraffic, Nonfelony Offense Waivers

Recruit Characteristic	Change in Percentage with Characteristic	Change in Man-Months Served	Annual Accessions Required	Reduction in Cost Per Accession	Potential Annual Cost Avoided
Tier 2	+5% points	–0.25	70,491	$2,667	$188M
Nontraffic offense misconduct waiver	+10% points	–0.10	70,202	$4,216	$296M

SOURCES: Study documented in Bruce R. Orvis, Christopher E. Maerzluft, Sung-Bou Kim, Michael G. Shanley, and Heather Krull, *Prospective Outcome Assessment for Alternative Recruit Selection Policies*, RAND Corporation, RR-2267-A, 2018. Reduction in cost per accession derived from ATRRS and HQDA G-1, FY 2018 data; David Knapp, Bruce R. Orvis, Christopher Maerzluft, and Tiffany Berglund, *Resources Required to Meet Army's Enlisted Recruiting Requirements Under Alternative Recruiting Goals, Conditions, and Eligibility Policies*, RAND Corporation, RR-2364-A, 2018.

NOTES: Actual results based on all Army enlistees from FY 2001–FY 2011. Confidence intervals not applicable to this population data. Change in man-months served refers to the change from an average of approximately 35 months served during the first term.

6.6: Cost-Effectiveness Analysis of the U.S. Army Assessment of Recruit Motivation and Strength (ARMS) Program (Niebuhr et al., 2013)

Description of the Study

This study compared morbidity (musculoskeletal injury), attrition rates, and related costs, of Army accessions who exceeded body fat (EBF) accession standards with those of weight-for-height or body-fat-qualified (WQ) recruits and, among the WQ subset, compared those who were physically fit as measured by the five-minute ARMS step test with those who had failed the test.

At the six Military Entrance Processing Stations employing the ARMS test, 11,639 WQ and 1,810 EBF study participants enlisted into the Army between February 2005 and September 2006. The study determined the probability-related costs of being EBF or WQ, passing or failing the step test, accessing or not, having musculoskeletal injuries or not, and attriting over time or not. It compared cost-effectiveness per year of service for WQ recruits against that for EBF recruits in the ARMS program and for WQ recruits who passed the ARMS step-test against that for those who failed the test.

RAND Arroyo Center Analysis

We focused on comparing the cost-effectiveness results for WQ and EBF recruits. The study reported that the cost per year of service for male recruits was $2,785 lower for WQ male recruits and $5,141 lower for WQ female recruits.

Next, we applied the estimated savings for a 70,000-accession mission of increasing waivers by 10 percentage points. From these savings, we needed to subtract the estimated incremental cost of the EBF recruits based on allowing 10 percent of the accessions to be EBF recruits who had passed the ARMS test. This required using the Niebuhr et al., 2013, results; weighting appropriately by the gender mix of the accessions (83.34 percent in the data underlying Table 6.8); and inflating the costs to 2018 dollars from 2013 dollars.

The gender-weighted difference in annual cost is $3,178, which becomes $3,426 in 2018 dollars. We then applied this incremental cost to 7,000 accessions (10 percent of the mission), which resulted in an incremental cost of $23,979,970 annually. The estimated savings based on Table 6.9 for increasing enlisted supply is $296 million, resulting in potential annual cost avoidance of approximately $272 million.

Table 6.9. Potential Annual Cost Avoided Due to Allowing EBF ARMS Recruits

Intervention	Annual Accessions	Percent EBF Through ARMS	Number Entering Through ARMS	Potential Annual Recruiting Costs Saved	Incremental Cost of ARMS Enlistees	Potential Annual Cost Avoided by Using ARMS
ARMS	70,000	10.00%	7,000	$296M	$24M	$272M

SOURCE: Study documented in David W. Niebuhr, William F. Page, David N. Cowan, Nadia Urban, Marlene E. Gubata, and Patrick Richard, "Cost-Effectiveness Analysis of the U.S. Army Assessment of Recruit Motivation and Strength (ARMS) Program," *Military Medicine*, Vol. 178, No. 10, 2013.
NOTE: Actual population results based on all Army enlistees during ARMS test. Confidence intervals not applicable to this population data.

Studies Involving the Use of Health Screenings to Reduce Alcohol Misuse and Alcohol-Related Behaviors

6.7: Screening for Alcohol Misuse and Alcohol-Related Behaviors Among Combat Veterans (Santiago et al., 2010)

Description of the Study

Health screenings of service members have been carried out three to six months after return from combat deployment. Three to four months after returning from deployment to Iraq, 6,527 U.S. Army soldiers completed anonymous surveys. A version of the Two-Item Conjoint Screen was included to screen for alcohol misuse. The objective of this study was to quantify the usefulness of the screening questions in predicting serious alcohol-related behaviors. Logistic regression was used to calculate the odds ratios for engaging in alcohol-related behaviors based on responses to the Two-Item Conjoint Screen alcohol screen, controlling for gender, rank, race, and active or reserve component. Twenty-seven percent of the soldiers screened positive for misusing alcohol. Soldiers screening positive were more likely to have recently engaged in illegal or work-related problem behaviors. All the adjusted odds ratios were on the order of 5 to 10: drinking and driving (4.99), reporting late or missing work (9.24), using illicit drugs (4.97), or being convicted of driving under the influence (4.84). Information on the incremental cost associated with these differences in problem behaviors was not available.

Although there is insufficient information to translate the benefits of using this screening test to assess the likelihood of predicting serious alcohol-related behaviors into cost avoidance, we include this study as an example of research with utility in screening service members to potentially avoid legal and work-related incidents with value in its own right.

Chapter 7. Health

This chapter presents information on the potential annual costs avoided associated with improved health outcomes. Table 7.1 categorizes the studies considered in this chapter, providing full titles and assigning study numbers.

Unless otherwise indicated, all effect sizes are in percentage points.

Table 7.1. Health Studies

Study Number	Name of Study
Studies Involving Training Programs Designed to Reduce Injuries Among All Recruits	
7.1	Effect of Pre-Accession Physical Fitness on Training Injuries Among US Army Recruits (Bedno et al., 2013)
7.2	The Victory Fitness Program: Influence of the US Army's Emerging Physical Readiness Training Doctrine on Fitness and Injuries in Basic Combat Training (Knapik et al., 2001)
7.3	Evaluation of Two Army Fitness Programs: The TRADOC Standardized Physical Training Program for Basic Combat Training and the Fitness Assessment Program (Injuries Among Standardized Group Participants) (Knapik, Darakjy, et al., 2004)
Studies Involving Training Programs Designed to Reduce Injuries Among Certain MOSs	
7.4	Influence of an Injury Reduction Program on Injury and Fitness Outcomes Among Soldiers (Knapik, Bullock, et al., 2004)
Studies of the Effect of an Alcohol Treatment Program on Duty Days	
7.5	Evaluation of a Four- Versus Six-week Length of Stay in the Navy's Alcohol Treatment Program (Trent, 1998)
Studies of Cost Savings Resulting from an Immunization Screening Program	
7.6	Cost-Minimization Analysis of the U.S. Army Accession Screening and Immunization Program (Tzeng, Jankosky, and Hughes, 2012)
Studies of Cost Savings Resulting from the Use of Telemedicine	
7.7	Utilization of Telemedicine in the U.S. Military in a Deployed Setting (Hwang et al., 2014)
7.8	A Cost Benefit of Telemedicine: An Assessment of Aero-Medical Evacuation Patients Throughout the Pacific Basin (Cornwell, 1995)
Studies of the Effectiveness of Suicide Prevention Programs	
7.9	Prevalence and Correlates of Suicidal Behavior Among Soldiers: Results from the Army Study to Assess Risk and Resilience in Service Members (Army STARRS) (Nock et al., 2014)
7.10	The US Air Force Suicide Prevention Program: Implications for Public Health Policy (Knox et al., 2010)

Studies Involving Training Programs Designed to Reduce Injuries Among All Recruits

7.1: Effect of Pre-Accession Physical Fitness on Training Injuries Among US Army Recruits (Bedno et al., 2013)

Description of the Study

This study examined the incidence of overuse injuries diagnosed during outpatient medical visits among a sample of male recruits who were administered the ARMS step test prior to military entry. The goal was to assess whether the ARMS was useful in identifying recruits with increased incidence of injury in the first 90 days of military service.

Among a sample of 8,456 study participants who enlisted in the Army between February 2005 and September 2006 at six Military Entrance Processing Stations, (1) 2,418 were diagnosed with an overuse injury in the first 90 days of service (28.60 incidence rate); (2) 6,511 passed the ARMS step test (77 percent); and 1,945 (23 percent) failed the test. Those who failed the ARMS step test were 31 percent more likely to experience an injury than those who passed.

RAND Arroyo Center Analysis

Using the ARMS pass rate, the overall incidence of overuse injury, and the adjusted hazard for injury, we first calculated the injury rates among those who passed and failed the ARMS step test: $0.77x + 0.23(1.31x) = 0.2860$, where $x = 0.2670$ is the injury rate among those who passed, and 0.3497 is the injury rate among those who failed ARMS (1.31 x0.2670).

Next, we calculated the injury reduction rate that would result from dropping 10 of the 23 percent of failing scorers on ARMS.[1] The overall ARMS failure rate then became 13 percent (23 percent minus 10 percent of the overall sample), and the pass rate became 87 percent. Using the new pass-fail rates and the injury incidence rates for both groups calculated in the previous paragraph, we estimated that, when these ARMS failers do not enter the military, the new overall injury incidence rate is 0.2778 ($0.87 \times 0.2670 + 0.13 \times 0.3497$), a reduction of 0.0082 (0.82 percentage points). We applied this percentage point reduction in the injury incidence rate to 70,000 annual accessions to calculate the number of potential annual injuries avoided. We then needed to multiply the number of potential annual injuries avoided by the cost per injury, which we describe next.

As discussed in Chapter 2, we used information from the Altarum Institute (2006) and an RMC calculator to estimate that a musculoskeletal injury costs $2,093 for an initial trainee. When the injury incidence rate is reduced by 0.82 percentage points and applied to 70,000 annual accessions, ARMS could potentially reduce the total number of annual injuries by 574. At

[1] Screening out the worst 6,000 would produce a bigger savings than a random 10-percent draw, although the calculations in the chart are consistent with a random draw.

a cost of $2,093 per injury, the potential annual costs avoided are $1.2 million. Table 7.2 summarizes the results.

Table 7.2. Potential Annual Cost Avoided Due to Reduced Injuries Following Participation in ARMS

	Reduction in Injury Incidence Rate	Annual Accessions	Potential Annual Injuries Avoided	Cost Per Injury	Potential Annual Cost Avoided
ARMS	0.82% [0.75%, 0.90%]	70,000	574 [526, 631]	$2,093	$1.2M [$1.1M, $1.3M]

SOURCES: Study documented in Sheryl A. Bedno, David N. Cowan, Nadia Urban, and David W. Niebuhr, "Effect of Pre-Accession Physical Fitness on Training Injuries Among US Army Recruits," *Work*, Vol. 44, No. 4, 201. Cost per injury derived from information provided in Altarum, Economic Analysis of Information Management Requirements, Injury Cause Coding, 2006.

7.2: The Victory Fitness Program: Influence of the US Army's Emerging Physical Readiness Training Doctrine on Fitness and Injuries in Basic Combat Training (Knapik et al., 2001)

Description of the Study

Around the time the study was written, the Army established the Physical Readiness Training (PRT) doctrine, which consisted of two training components, toughening and conditioning. As part of the toughening phase, the Army established a program called Victory Fitness. Part of the program involved screening individual medical records for information on injuries. One of the goals of this study was to compare the injury rates among service members who had participated in the Victory Fitness program with those for a control group that conducted a traditional BCT physical training program.

A Cox regression comparing overuse injuries between Victory Fitness program participants and members of the control group found an adjusted risk ratio of 1.57 for men in the control group and an adjusted risk ratio of 1.45 for women (Table 21). The study also reported cumulative overuse injury rates of 15.4 and 42.7 percent for men and women, respectively, in the control group.

RAND Arroyo Center Analysis

We calculated the reciprocal of the adjusted risk ratios from the Cox regression (1 / 1.57 = 0.64 for men, and 1 / 1.45 = 0.69 for women) and combined them into a single rate using the gender distribution of the FY 2017 accession cohort of 83.25 percent men, 16.75 percent women ($0.64 \times 0.8325 + 0.69 \times 0.1675 = 0.65$). We used the same gender distribution to calculate a single overuse incidence rate for the control group of 19.97 percent ($15.4 \times 0.8325 + 42.7 \times 0.1675$). Applying the adjusted risk ratio to the injury incidence rate, we calculated a modified injury rate of 12.90 percent (19.97×0.65). We then multiplied the difference in injury rates (19.97 percent minus 12.90 percent = 7.07 percentage points) by a 70,000-person accession cohort to estimate the number of injuries saved by the Victory Fitness program (70,000 × 0.707), or 4,952 fewer injuries. We then multiplied the total number of potential injuries avoided by the cost of an injury ($2,093).

The Victory Fitness program involved a 32-hour block of instruction to drill sergeants who, in turn, trained soldiers in BCT. We estimated the cost of one day of classroom training to be $1,046 (see Chapter 2). The estimated cost for each drill sergeant trained in this program was $4,185. We applied a ratio of drill sergeants to BCT trainees of 1:80 (see Chapter 2) to a full accession cohort. This results in a program cost of $3,661,713 (70,000 / 80 × $4,185) in FY 2017 dollars. Inflated to FY 2018 dollars, the cost of the program is $3,745,089.

With 4,952 fewer injuries, each of which would have cost $2,093, we estimated the potential annual costs avoided from participating in the Victory Fitness program as $10,360,389. The cost of the running the program is $3,745,089, resulting in estimated net potential annual cost avoided of $6,615,300. Table 7.3 presents the key information.

Table 7.3. Potential Annual Cost Avoided Due to Fewer Injuries Following Participation in the Victory Fitness Program

	Reduction in Injury Rate	Annual Accessions	Potential Annual Injuries Avoided	Cost Per Injury	Potential Annual Cost Avoided from Reduction in the Number of Injuries	Cost of Running Victory Fitness Program	Potential Annual Cost Avoided
Victory Fitness Program	7.07% [5.22%, 9.41%]	70,000	4,952 [3,657, 6,593]	$2,093	$10.4M [$7,651,975, $13,794,578]	$3,745,089	$6.6M [$3.9M, $10.0M]

SOURCES: Study documented in J. J. Knapik, K. Hauret, J. M. Bednarek, S. Arnold, M. Canham-Chervak, A. Mansfield, E. Hoedebecke, J. Mancuso, T. L. Barker, D. Duplessis, H. Heckel, J. Peterson, and the Staff of the US Army Physical Fitness School in the Year 2001, *The Victory Fitness Program: Influence of the US Army's Emerging Physical Readiness Training Doctrine on Fitness and Injuries in Basic Combat Training*, U.S. Army Center for Health Promotion and Preventive Medicine, July 2001. Cost per injury derived from information provided in Altarum, Economic Analysis of Information Management Requirements, Injury Cause Coding, 2006.

7.3: Evaluation of Two Army Fitness Programs: The TRADOC Standardized Physical Training Program for Basic Combat Training and the Fitness Assessment Program (Injuries Among Standardized Group Participants) (Knapik, Darakjy, et al., 2004)

Description of the Study

To attempt to reduce injuries and attrition from BCT, the Army developed a standardized physical training program. This study evaluated the effectiveness of the program by comparing two groups, the SG that implemented the new training program, and the NSG that implemented the traditional BCT physical training program.

According to Table 28 of the study, the relative risk of an overuse injury in the NSG compared with the SG, after adjusting for age, Body Mass Index, and three APFT events, is 1.40

for men and 1.43 for women. The study also reported (in Table 24) that the person-time overuse injury incidence rates (measured as number of overuse injuries per 1,000 trainee-days) is 3.51 for men in the NSG and 7.71 for women in the NSG.

RAND Arroyo Center Analysis

We inverted the risk ratios (1 / 1.4 = 0.71 for men and 1 / 1.43 = 0.70 for women) and combined the risk ratios for men and women into a single ratio using the gender distribution from the FY 2017 accession cohort, which is 0.71 (0.71 × 0.8325 + 0.70 × 0.16.75). A risk ratio of 0.71 represents a reduction of 29 percent. We also combined the gender-specific NSG overuse injury incidence rates into a single rate (3.51 × 0.8325 + 7.71 × 0.1675 = 4.21). The incidence rate is reported as the number of overuse injuries per 1,000 trainee-days; therefore, to calculate the total number of injuries among the SG in a year, we first converted a 70,000-person accession cohort into trainee days per 1,000: 70,000 × 63 / 1,000 = 4,410 (the factor of 63 represents the number of days a trainee spends in BCT). We then multiplied the total number of trainee days (divided by 1,000) by the gender-weighted incidence rate: 4,410 × 4.21 = 18,581 total overuse injuries among NSG participants per year. Using the gender-weighted risk ratio, the total number of overuse injuries among SG participants is 18,581 × 0.71 = 13,225. The difference between these two estimates of the number of overuse injuries per year—5,356—represents the potential annual injuries avoided by participating in the SG, which we multiplied by the cost of an overuse (musculoskeletal) injury ($2,093).

The program requires 16 hours of classroom training for drill sergeants. Based on a $1,046 cost of one day of classroom training and a drill sergeant-to-soldier ratio of 1:80 for a full accession cohort, this results in a program cost of $1,872,545 in FY 2018 dollars.

The reduction in the number of annual injuries created by participating in the SG (5,356) multiplied by the cost of an injury ($2,093) produces estimated savings of $11,204,015. The cost of running the program ($1,872,545) is subtracted, resulting in estimated potential annual net cost avoidance of $9,331,471. Unlike the attrition results presented in the earlier discussion of this program (Study 3.16), potential savings resulting from lower rates of injuries exceed estimated program costs. See Table 7.4.

Table 7.4. Potential Annual Cost Avoided Due to Fewer Injuries Among Standardized Group Participants

Intervention	Reduction in Injury Rate[a]	Total Number of BCT Trainee Days[b]	Injury Rate per 1,000 Trainee Days for NSG	Total Number of Potential Annual Injuries Avoided	Cost Per Injury	Potential Annual Cost Avoided from Reduction in the Number of Injuries	Cost of Running SG Program	Potential Annual Cost Avoided
SG	29% [21.88%, 38.39%]	4,410	4.21	5,356 [4,041, 7,090]	$2,093	$11,204,015 [$8,453,499, $14,831,700]	$1,872,545	$9.3M [$6.6M, $13.0M]

SOURCES: Study documented in Joseph J. Knapik, Salima Darakjy, Shawn Scott, Keith G. Hauret, Sara Canada, Roberto Marin, Frank Palkoska, Steven VanCamp, Eugene Piskator, William Rieger, and Bruce H. Jones, *Evaluation of Two Army Fitness Programs: The TRADOC Standardized Physical Training Program for Basic Combat Training and the Fitness Assessment Program*, Army Center for Health Promotion and Preventive Medicine, February 2004.

[a] Per 1,000 trainee days.

[b] Divided by 1,000.

Studies Involving Training Programs Designed to Reduce Injuries Among Certain MOSs

7.4: Influence of an Injury Reduction Program on Injury and Fitness Outcomes Among Soldiers (Knapik, Bullock, et al., 2004)

Description of the Study

This study compared injury rates among soldiers attending Ordnance AIT at Aberdeen Proving Ground who went through PRT, a multiple-intervention program that was aimed at reducing training injuries with the rates for a historical control group that participated in the traditional physical training program. PRT program elements included three interventions: (1) 32 hours of field instruction on exercises provided to drill sergeants, who subsequently administered the program to soldiers; (2) a seven-hour injury control classroom education course administered to unit staff and student trainers; and (3) individual soldier data entry (including name, type of injury, body part, activity associated with injury, and type and length of activity restriction) into the Unit Based Injury Surveillance System (UBISS).

The study reported control group injury rates of 7.5 per 100 person-months for men and 13.4 for women. For the multiple-intervention group, injury rates were 6.7 per 100 person-months for men and 9.7 for women. Therefore, trainees who participated in the PRT experienced lower injury rates, a reduction of 0.8 and 3.7 per 100 person-month, for men and women, respectively.

RAND Arroyo Center Analysis

Using personnel files, we computed a gender mix of 89.38 percent men and 10.62 percent women among recent ordnance recruits, analogous to the ones studied earlier (wheeled vehicle mechanic [91B], small arms/towed artillery repairer [91F], track vehicle repairer [91H], self-propelled artillery systems maintainer [91P], and Stryker systems maintainer [91S]), between FYs 2016 and 2018. That mix produces a gender-weighted reduction in injury rate of 1.1079 ($0.8 \times 0.8938 + 3.7 \times 0.1062$). We applied that rate to the estimated number of annual ordnance AIT trainees for the MOS listed above (4,153), based on the average from FYs 2016–2018, accounting for the fact that each trainee is in AIT for three months. We then divided by 100 to apply the difference in the gender-weighted injury rate per 100 person-months. This results in 138 fewer injuries. We multiplied the reduction in the number of injuries by the cost per injury ($2,093; see Chapter 2 and Study 7.1) to estimate the potential Annual Costs Avoided as a result of a reduction in injuries among PRT participants.

Next, we calculated the cost of administering PRT. For the 32 hours of *field* instruction provided to drill sergeants, we prorated an average drill instructor's salary for four days of work. The characteristics we applied were E-6, 10 years of service, married and filing jointly, and living in an average cost area (Colorado Springs, Colorado), corresponding to an RMC of

$71,250.30. We assumed 260 days in a work year, which means four days of training cost $1,096.16 per drill sergeant. We assumed that, once a drill sergeant has been trained, he or she would be able to instruct three groups of AIT soldiers per year (our ordnance AIT lasts about 13 weeks). If the typical drill sergeant-to-soldier ratio is 1:40 for AIT and three classes of AIT could be taught, we apply a ratio of 1:120, resulting in an annual cost of $37,936 to provide field instruction to drill sergeants for the annual number of ordnance AIT trainees.

The second component of PRT consists of seven hours of classroom training administered to unit staff and student trainers. We used the same average daily cost for these individuals as we discussed in Chapter 2 ($1,046.20 per day). Prorated to seven hours, the average cost of participating in this classroom training is $915.43. Again assuming a ratio of one unit staff or student trainer to 40 soldiers, with three AIT cohorts trained once the unit staff or student trainer receives classroom training (therefore, a ratio of 1:120), the cost of training enough unit staff or student trainers for the annual number of ordnance AIT trainees in the selected MOS is $32,403 in FY 2018 dollars.

Finally, to calculate the cost of entering injury data into UBISS, we first estimated the number of annual injuries and then multiplied by the prorated salary spent on each entry. We used the multiple-intervention group injury rates to calculate the number of injuries an accession cohort would experience per year. As noted, Ordnance AIT lasts 13 weeks, which means each recruit contributes three person-months. We converted 4,153 Ordnance AIT trainees (the number of annual ordnance accessions at the time of our study, according to the Army's Regular Army Analyst) to "per 100 person-months," which is the unit used to report injury rates (4,153 × 3 / 100 = 124.59). Applying the gender ratio from above, this splits into 111 men and 13 women and an estimated 874 injuries per year across the accession cohort (111 × 6.7 = 746 for men and 13 × 9.7 = 128 for women). We calculated an average RMC of $58,481 for an E-4 or E-5 doing data entry. We assumed that each entry would take four minutes, resulting in a per-injury cost of $1.87 ($58,481 over 260 days, with each day lasting 480 minutes, multiplied by four minutes per entry). Entering 874 injuries in UBISS would cost $1,639.

Therefore, the cost of administering PRT is the sum of the cost of the three components: (1) $37,936 for drill sergeant field instruction; (2) $32,403 for unit staff or student trainer classroom instruction; and (3) $1,639 for data entry into UBISS, totaling $71,978.

The estimated potential cost avoided resulting from fewer injuries among PRT participants is the reduction in injuries multiplied by the cost per injury, or 138 × 2,093 = $288,791. From this, we subtracted the cost of administering PRT ($71,978), which results in estimated net potential annual cost avoidance of $216,813, as shown in Table 7.5.

Table 7.5. Potential Annual Cost Avoided as a Result of Participating in the Physical Readiness Training Multiple Intervention Program

	Reduction in Injury Rate (per 100 person-months)	Number of Annual AIT Trainees	Number of Months per Trainee	Potential Annual Injuries Avoided	Cost Per Injury	Potential Annual Cost Avoided from a Reduction in the Number of Injuries	Cost of Administering PRT	Potential Annual Cost Avoided
PRT	1.11% [0.86%, 1.38%]	4,153	3	138 [107, 172]	$2,093	$288,791 [$224,226, $359,363]	$71,978	$0.2M [$0.2M, $0.3M]

SOURCES: Study documented in J. J. Knapik, S. H. Bullock, S. Canada, E. Toney, J. D. Wells, E. Hoedebecke, and B. H. Jones, "Influence of an Injury Reduction Program on Injury and Fitness Outcomes Among Soldiers," *Injury Prevention*, Vol. 10, No. 1, February 2004. Cost per injury derived from information provided in Altarum, Economic Analysis of Information Management Requirements, Injury Cause Coding, 2006.

Studies of the Effect of an Alcohol Treatment Program on Duty Days

7.5: Evaluation of a Four- Versus Six-Week Length of Stay in the Navy's Alcohol Treatment Program (Trent, 1998)

Description of the Study

The purpose of the study was to determine whether reducing the length of a Navy alcohol inpatient treatment program from six weeks to four would have adverse effects. Over a 28-month period from February 1992 to May 1994, 2,923 participants volunteered to participate in the study, representing 91 percent of all eligible incoming patients.

Across the seven outcomes measured (alcohol use; negative incidents, such as alcohol-related work absences or legal and/or disciplinary actions; retention on active duty; undesirable discharge; job performance; recommended for reenlistment or advancement; and self-reported quality of life), the length of the program never had a significant impact, controlling for demographic characteristics, personal background, clinical profile, and treatment variables.

RAND Arroyo Center Analysis

Because reducing the length of the program from six weeks to four did not result in worse outcomes, we computed cost savings as the additional two weeks of duty time that are gained if the service member is discharged to return to duty earlier. This estimate is conservative because it is net of the inpatient costs associated with treating the patient for the longer period. The Navy program had 3,212 admissions over a 28-month period (1,377 per year) on average. Using active-duty end strength from 2014 for the Navy (325,400), that implies a participation rate of 0.42 percent. If the same program were implemented in the Army, this would translate into 2,063 participants using the Army's FY 2019 end strength (487,500). Using the same average soldier assumptions from Study 7.1 (RMC of $58,490.95) and 260 workdays per year, the daily compensation rate is $224.97 ($58,490.95 / 260), or $2,249.65 over ten workdays from the two-week reduction in the length of the program.

If the Army had a similar six-week alcohol inpatient program that could be reduced from six weeks to four weeks without negatively affecting outcomes, we estimate that the change could generate $4,641,032 in potential annual costs avoided by getting service members back to duty more quickly. Table 7.6 summarizes our results.

Table 7.6. Potential Annual Cost Avoided Due to a Reduction in the Length of the Navy's Alcohol Treatment Program

Intervention	Reduction in Length of Program	Average Daily Compensation	Annual Number of Program Participants	Potential Annual Cost Avoided
Reduced length of inpatient alcohol treatment program	10 days	$224.97	2,063	$4.6M

SOURCES: Study documented in L. K. Trent, "Evaluation of a Four- Versus Six-Week Length of Stay in the Navy's Alcohol Treatment Program," *Journal of Studies on Alcohol*, Vol. 59, No. 3, 1998.
NOTE: Actual results based on all program participants. Confidence intervals not applicable to these population data.

Studies of Cost Savings Resulting from an Immunization Screening Program

7.6: Cost-Minimization Analysis of the U.S. Army Accession Screening and Immunization Program (Tzeng, Jankosky, and Hughes, 2012)

Description of the Study

Until 2005, the Army universally administered the measles, mumps, and rubella; hepatitis A; and hepatitis B vaccines to all recruits without screening for preexisting immunity. In 2005, the Army instituted a new program, the Accession Screening and Immunization Program (ASIP), to ensure the highest level of immunity against hepatitis A, hepatitis B, measles, rubella, and varicella, with the goal of reducing overall vaccination costs. The purpose of this study was to conduct a cost-minimization analysis between the universal immunization program and the ASIP.

Using data on 41,164 recruits who entered Ft. Leonard Wood between October 1, 2007, and September 30, 2009, the study showed that ASIP saved the Army $410,562 relative to the cost of the universal immunization program ($1,504,587 compared with $1,094,025). This results in an average savings of $9.97 per recruit in 2011 dollars, which inflates to $11.09 in 2018.

RAND Arroyo Center Analysis

We multiplied the total number of recruits in a given accession cohort (70,000) by the average cost savings per recruit from using the ASIP. Estimated potential annual costs avoided total $776,300 (70,000 × 11.09), as shown in Table 7.7.

Table 7.7. Cost-Minimization Analysis of the U.S. Army Accession Screening and Immunization Program

Screener	Annual Accessions	Savings Per Recruit	Potential Annual Cost Avoided
ASIP	70,000	$11.09	$0.8M

SOURCES: Study documented in Jeff Tzeng, Christopher Jankosky, and Hayley Hughes, "Cost-Minimization Analysis of the U.S. Army Accession Screening and Immunization Program," *Military Medicine*, Vol. 177, No. 2, December 2012.
NOTE: Actual results based on all program participants. Confidence intervals not applicable to these population data.

Studies of Cost Savings Resulting from the Use of Telemedicine

7.7: Utilization of Telemedicine in the U.S. Military in a Deployed Setting (Hwang et al., 2014)

Description of the Study

In 2004, the U.S. Army Medical Department established a centralized telemedicine program. This study analyzed teledermatology consultations that occurred between 2004 and 2012 to assess volume, response time, and medical evacuation status. Between April 2004 and December 2012, there were 4,379 teledermatology consultations, most of which originated from Iraq and Afghanistan. Of those, 46 dermatalogic evacuations were avoided. Over this period (eight years, nine months), the average was 5.26 evacuations per year.

RAND Arroyo Center Analysis

We multiplied the average number of evacuations per year by the cost of an evacuation, $24,000, which we obtained from Rand et al., 2009. Inflated to 2018 dollars, this becomes $28,086. At 5.26 medical evacuations avoided per year and $28,086 per evacuation, this results in estimated total potential annual costs avoided of $147,652, as shown in Table 7.8. The incremental cost of the teledermatology consultations, if any, is unknown.

Table 7.8. Utilization of Telemedicine in the U.S. Military in a Deployed Setting

	Medical Evacuations Avoided per Year	Cost of a Medical Evacuation	Potential Annual Cost Avoided
Telemedicine	5.26	$28,086	$0.1M

SOURCES: Study documented in Jane S. Hwang, Charles M. Lappan, Leonard C. Sperling, and Jon H. Meyerle, "Utilization of Telemedicine in the U.S. Military in a Deployed Setting," *Military Medicine*, Vol. 179, No. 11, 2014. Medical evacuation cost estimate from Rand et al., 2009.
NOTE: Actual results based on all program participants. Confidence intervals not applicable to this population data.

7.8: A Cost Benefit of Telemedicine: An Assessment of Aero-Medical Evacuation Patients Throughout the Pacific Basin (Cornwell, 1995)

Description of the Study

In 1993, Tripler Army Medical Center began providing televideo consultations to overseas military installations. The purpose of this study was to estimate the cost avoidance that telemedicine can produce by evaluating or treating patients remotely rather than medically evacuating them. The study analyzed medical evacuation data from seven installations to Tripler Army Medical Center in 1993 to determine which could have been avoided if telemedicine had been used.

From the seven installations studied, there were 2,156 medical evacuations during FY 1993. One of those seven installations was Army, representing 168 (7.79 percent) evacuations. Using the Delphi technique, experts believe 780 of the 2,156 patients could have been treated via telemedicine if the system were available. Assuming the same service proportions of potential saved medevacs as among total actual medevacs, the Army may have avoided 61 medevacs (7.79 percent of 780) if telemedicine could have been used.

RAND Arroyo Center Analysis

We again multiplied the estimated cost of a medevac from Rand et al., 2009, inflated to 2018 dollars ($28,086) by the estimated number of potential Army medevacs saved (61). As shown in Table 7.9, estimated potential annual costs avoided for the potential 61 saved medevacs were $1,707,045. The incremental cost of the telemedicine consultations, if any, is unknown.

Table 7.9. Potential Annual Cost Avoided Resulting from Using Telemedicine to Reduce Aero-Medical Evacuations in the Pacific Basin

	Potential Medevacs Avoided Across All Sites	Percentage of Total Medevacs from Army Installation	Potential Army Medevacs Avoided	Medevac Cost	Potential Annual Cost Avoided
Telemedicine	780	7.79	61	$28,086	$1.7M

SOURCES: Study documented in Dan Cornwell, *A Cost Benefit of Telemedicine: An Assessment of Aero-Medical Evacuation Patients Throughout the Pacific Basin*, Academy of Health Sciences (Army), Health Care Administration, 1995. Medical evacuation cost estimate from Rand et al., 2009.
NOTE: Actual results based on all program participants. Confidence intervals not applicable to this population data.

Studies of the Effectiveness of Suicide Prevention Programs

7.9: Prevalence and Correlates of Suicidal Behavior Among Soldiers: Results from the Army Study to Assess Risk and Resilience in Service Members (Army STARRS) (Nock et al., 2014)

Description of the Study

In recent years, the suicide rate among U.S. soldiers has increased rapidly, while the civilian suicide rate has remained stable. This study examines the relationships between mental disorders and suicide attempts from a nine-month cross section (April to December 2011) of active-duty Army personnel.

The lifetime prevalence of suicide attempts in the cross-section was 2.4 percent. Among those with a lifetime suicide attempt, 53 percent had postenlistment onset. The number of people in the study sample was 5,324. Intermittent explosive disorder had the highest preenlistment prevalence (15.5 percent) among all the mental disorders considered for this sample, with an association with a postenlistment suicide attempt (odds ratio) of 3.9.

RAND Arroyo Center Analysis

Based on the detailed numbers just summarized, the prevalence of a postenlistment attempted suicide among the 5,324 enlistees in the sample is 1.27734 percent. Using this information, we determined the number of people with and without intermittent explosive disorder who had attempted suicide. The odds ratio of 3.9 equals the number of postenlistment attempted suicides among those with A preenlistment disorder (0.155 times 5,324) divided by the remainder of the preenlistment disorder group, which is then divided by the number of postenlistment attempted suicides among those without preenlistment disorder (0.845 times 5,324) divided by the remainder of the preenlistment group without a diagnosis of intermittent explosive disorder.

The resulting estimates are that 40 people without the disorder had suicide attempts postenlistment and that 28 people with the disorder made a postenlistment attempt, rates of 0.889 percent and 3.394 percent, respectively. Next, we calculated what decrease in postenlistment suicide attempts could be achieved if the Army screened out 10 percent of recruits with the disorder. The resulting composition of accessions would be $15.50 - 1.55 = 13.95$ percent with the disorder and 86.05 percent without the disorder. Using these percentages and the attempted suicide rates calculated above, we estimate that the new postenlistment suicide attempt rate would be 1.23898 percent ($0.8605 \times 0.00894 + 0.1395 \times 0.03368$), a reduction of 0.03836 percentage points ($1.27734 - 1.23898$). We estimated that, if the Army screened recruits on the presence of the disorder, it might be possible to reduce the number of postenlistment suicide attempts by 27 among an accession cohort of 70,000, as shown in Table 7.10. A reduction in the number of suicides is considered a value in its own right, so we did not attempt to quantify the cost savings associated with screening on intermittent explosive disorder.

Table 7.10. Prevalence and Correlates of Suicidal Behavior Among Soldiers

	Reduction in Suicide Attempt Rate	Annual Accessions	Potential Annual Suicides Avoided
Intermittent explosive disorder	3.89×10^{-2}% [0.02%, 0.06%]	70,000	27 [13, 43]

SOURCE: Study documented in Matthew K. Nock, Murray B. Stein, Steven G. Heeringa, Robert J. Ursano, Lisa J. Colpe, Carol S. Fullerton, Irving Hwang, James A. Naifeh, Nancy A. Sampson, Michael Schoenbaum, Alan M. Zaslavsky, and Ronald C. Kessler, "Prevalence and Correlates of Suicidal Behavior Among Soldiers: Results from the Army Study to Assess Risk and Resilience in Service Members (Army STARRS)," *JAMA Psychiatry*, Vol. 71, No. 5, May 2014.

7.10: The US Air Force Suicide Prevention Program: Implications for Public Health Policy (Knox et al., 2010)

Description of the Study

The study examined the effectiveness of the U.S. Air Force Suicide Prevention Program (AFSPP) in reducing suicides. AFSPP was launched in 1996 and focuses on reducing suicide through early identification and treatment of those at risk. The authors used 27 years of data, from 1981 through 2008, representing 16 years of data before the AFSPP was launched and 11 years of data after, and used regression analysis to evaluate the influence of the AFSPP on quarterly suicide rates over time.

Prior to the launch of the AFSPP in 1996, the estimated mean suicide rate per quarter was 3.033 per 100,000 airmen. After the program was launched, the estimated mean was 2.387 per 100,000, a difference of 0.646 per 100,000 airmen per quarter.

RAND Arroyo Center Analysis

Using the authors' estimate of 0.646 per 100,000 airmen per quarter saved due to a reduction in the suicide rate owing to the AFSPP, we calculated how many soldiers could be saved if this program were implemented in the Army. We used the 2019 active-duty total strength of 487,500 authorized in the National Defense Act and estimate that 13 suicides could be avoided (487,500 / 100,000 × 0.646 × 4 quarters) (Pub. L. 115-232, 2018, Section 401). Table 7.11 summarizes the estimation.

Table 7.11. The US Air Force Suicide Prevention Program: Implications for Public Health Policy

Screener	Active-Duty Total Strength (2018)	Suicide Reduction Rate	Potential Annual Suicides Avoided
AFSPP	487,500	0.646 per 100,000 per quarter	13

SOURCE: Study documented in Kerry L. Knox, Steven Pflanz, Gerald W. Talcott, Rick L. Campise, Jill E. Lavigne, Alina Bajorska, Xin Tu, and Eric D. Caine, "The US Air Force Suicide Prevention Program: Implications for Public Health Policy," *American Journal of Public Health*, Vol. 100, No. 12, 2010.
NOTE: Confidence intervals not applicable to this population data.

Chapter 8. Overview of Our Research and Its Implications

Senior leaders often understand the relevance of behavioral and social science research but are not able to compare its value with the benefits of operational programs or other types of research using similar metrics. The purpose of our research was to translate outcomes often reported in behavioral and social science research studies into estimates of the value of the outcomes in metrics that senior leaders can readily understand and use to compare benefits across different screeners, interventions, or other factors and outcomes, such as their implications for potential cost avoidance or other benefits. This report discussed the selected outcomes, their linkage to the benefits identified, utility function development and methodology, and the application of the resulting utility functions to illustrative research studies across different types of outcomes and study factors.

Interpreting the Results in This Report

Estimates of these benefits and of the implications for potential cost avoidance for the studies discussed in this report were made independently for each study. The estimates are of the benefit(s) of the screener(s), intervention(s), or other factor(s) discussed in each study, given recent Army conditions, such as accession; attrition and reenlistment rates; and recruiting, training and bonus costs, all else equal. The study write-ups of specific factors do not attempt to analyze the benefits of combining factors across studies, in part because the data required for such combinations (e.g., covariation between the factors) were generally not available. Analogously, for similar reasons, such as the need for data on the covariation between the factors and all relevant current Army policies, the write-ups do not attempt to assess the incremental benefit of applying the factors discussed in a study in the current environment. Therefore, the write-ups are not recommendations to implement the screeners, interventions, or other factors.

Finally, as we mention in Chapter 2, our analyses did not account for several costs, such as increases in recruiting costs when certain screening measures are used (e.g., those needing waivers), costs associated with administering and evaluating psychological screening measures, and the cost of conducting these types of social science studies. We believe these costs are significantly smaller than the potential cost savings found in our analyses. In addition, we could not include cost savings from studies that produced small or statistically insignificant effects and are therefore not found in the literature. We have multiple studies on related outcomes with highly significant results, so the likelihood that the results were achieved by chance is quite small.

Implications of Our Analysis for Future Behavioral Science Research

Ideally, research should report results that can be directly used to estimate the effect of a screener or other intervention on the outcome of interest, such as a complete set of regression-based results or actual results for categorical predictors. For researchers interested in maximizing the extent to which their work can be interpreted by and for policymakers, we recommend providing these data in future work. However, while many of the studies we summarized in this report provide all the necessary data, others do not. As we have shown, methods were available in some of these cases that allowed us to estimate the effect on the outcome. These methods should be considered a less-preferable backup.

We found evidence of the success of certain screeners, interventions, and other factors in reducing legal incidents or adverse medical outcomes. For example, we identified interventions that reduced bad conduct discharges, demotions, drug-related discharges, punitive discharges, and health care utilization. However, we were unable to identify available cost measures for these outcomes. Consequently, additional research in these areas could be useful for quantifying return on investment relating to legal and medical screeners, interventions, or other factors and their outcomes.

Appendix A. Inputs to Calculations

This chapter contains information on how costs were derived for several outcomes and programs throughout this report, including

- BCT, OSUT, and IET costs
- pilot training.

Derivation of IET-Related Training Cost Metrics

Table A.1 summarizes the accession (including USMEPCOM costs) and training costs used in this report, followed in the rest of this section by a description of their sources and derivation. The basic inputs are the cost of accession and the cost per graduate for certain types of courses, as well as the attrition rate for those courses. The most commonly used cost factors are "cost per IET graduate" and "cost per BCT graduate." The base information is for FY 2017 training, and the costs are in FY 2018 dollars.

Table A.1. Summary of BCT, AIT, OSUT, and IET Costs

Summary Cost Item	Cost per Graduate	Cost per Enrollee	Cost to Replace Graduate
Accession	$27,137	N/A	N/A
BCT	$18,250	$16,973	$47,430
AIT	$33,000	$31,350	$82,926
OSUT	$30,350	$27,012	$60,841
IET			$75,638

NOTE: Cost per enrollee and cost to replace graduate take into account attrition.

Inputs and Derivation of Basic Cost Factors

The most basic inputs come from the MPA annual information paper which lists the following basic costs shown in Table A.2.

We took the basic cost metrics and derived summary cost items for the cost of accession, BCT, AIT, and OSUT. The costs in Table A.3 represent cost per graduate.

For some studies, the cost per enrollee was needed as opposed to the cost per graduate. We derived the cost per enrollee from attrition rate information for each of the course types, as shown in Table A.4.

Table A.2. Inputs to Army Training Cost Metrics

Number	Item	Cost
1	Cost per accession	$25,337
2	Cost for processing through USMEPCOM	$1,800
3	BCT TRADOC training cost per graduate	$17,600
4	AIT TRADOC training cost per graduate	$33,000
5	OSUT TRADOC training cost per graduate	$29,700
6	Recruiting Battalion cost	$650

SOURCE: MPA, October 2018.

Table A.3. Computation of Cost per Graduate or Accession

Summary Cost Item	Amount	Source
Accession	$27,137	(1) + (2)
BCT	$18,250	(3) + (6)
AIT	$33,000	(4)
OSUT	$30,350	(5) + (6)

NOTE: Numbers in parentheses refers to row numbers in Table A.2

Table A.4. Computation of Cost per Enrollee

Summary Cost Item	Cost per Graduate (a)	Attrition Rate (b)	Cost per Enrollee {(a) × [(1.0) – (b)]}
BCT	$18,250	7.0%	$16,973
AIT	$33,000	5.0%	$31,350
OSUT	$30,350	11.0%	$27,012

NOTE: Attrition rates derived from ATRRS data and from *p* factors of TRADOC's ATRM-159 analysis in 2017.

Derivation of Replacement Cost Per Graduate Factors

In many instances, our analyses called for a replacement cost per graduate, which required determining what it would cost to access a new soldier and take him or her through all the required training to a given point (e.g., through AIT). This requires taking into account not only the cost of the latest course but also the cost of previous courses taken, the attrition rates in those courses, and the cost of accession. Because of attrition in courses, the replacement cost exceeds the sum of the costs of individual courses plus the cost of accession.

In the following subsections, we derive the cost of replacing a BCT graduate, an AIT graduate, an OSUT graduate, and an IET graduate.

BCT Cost

The cost of replacing a BCT graduate is the cost per graduate of the BCT course plus the cost of 1.075 accessions. The latter figure takes into account that 7 percent of accessions do not graduate from BCT. See Table A.5 for the calculations.

Table A.5. Cost of BCT

Summary Cost Item	Cost per Graduate (a)	Attrition Rate (b)	Number to Replace (c)	Calculation of Number to Replace	Cost by Item (a) × (c)
Accession	$27,137		1.075	= 1 / (1 – 0.07)	$29,180
BCT	$18,250	7.0%	1.000	N/A	$18,250
Total cost to replace					$47,430

AIT Cost

The cost of replacing an AIT graduate is the cost per graduate of the AIT course plus the cost of 1.053 graduates of the BCT course plus the cost of 1.132 accessions. The figures take into account that 7 percent of accessions do not graduate from BCT and that 5 percent of the BCT graduates do not graduate from AIT. Table A.6 shows the calculations.

Table A.6. Cost of AIT

Summary Cost Item	Cost per Graduate (a)	Attrition Rate (b)	Number to Replace (c)	Calculation of Number to Replace	Cost by Item (a) × (c)
Accession	$27,137		1.132	= 1.053/(1 – 0.07)	$30,715
BCT	$18,250	7.0%	1.053	= 1/(1 – 0.05)	$19,211
AIT	$33,000	5.0%	1.000	N/A	$33,000
Total cost to replace					$82,926

OSUT Cost

The cost of replacing an OSUT graduate is the cost per graduate of the OSUT course plus the cost of 1.123 accessions. The latter figure takes into account that 11 percent of accessions do not graduate from OSUT. See Table A.7 for the calculations.

Table A.7. Cost of OSUT

Summary Cost Item	Cost per Graduate (a)	Attrition Rate (b)	Number to Replace (c)	Calculation of Number to Replace	Cost by Item (a) × (c)
Accession	$27,137		1.124	= 1.000 / (1 – 0.11)	$30,491
OSUT	$30,350	11.0%	1.000	N/A	$30,350
Total cost to replace					$60,841

IET Cost

The replacement cost of an IET graduate is a weighted average of OSUT and AIT cost. The proportion OSUT of all enrollees is about 33 percent (ATRRS, 2017). Thus, the replacement cost of IET is $75,638 [$60,841 × 0.33 + $82,926 × (1 – 0.33)].

Pilot Training

According to the DA FY 2019 budget estimates, average number of students entering advanced graduate flight training for fixed-wing aircraft in FYs 2017–2019 was 108 (DA, 2018). Cowan, Barrett, and Wegner, 1990, had a sample of 1,124 UPT completions and 282 UNT completions. Therefore, approximately one-quarter as many people completed navigator training as completed pilot training. We used this ratio to estimate that the Army would have had 25 students in navigator training.

We used TRADOC's ATRM-159 report to calculate the cost of completing C-12 aviator qualification. The attrition rate for C-12 aviator qualification training is low (1 percent), which may be explained by the fact that a fixed-wing aviator in the Army must be qualified in rotary training before entering the fixed-wing course. Using a 1 percent attrition rate and the information in ATRM-159, we estimated the cost of a graduate of C-12 aviator qualification (FY 2017 training) to be $221,698 (FY 2018 dollars).

For some studies, we needed to know the cost of navigator training. Air Force fixed-wing pilot training consists of 40 days of Initial Flight Screening, followed by approximately one year of SUPT or nine months of UNT. We prorated the full cost of pilot training ($221,698) for studies examining Initial Flight Screening as follows: 1 1/3 months divided by 13 1/3 months, multiplied by $221,698 = $22,170. For UNT, we used 10 1/3 months divided by 13 1/3 months, multiplied by $221,698 =$171,816.

Appendix B. Derivation of Special Forces–Related Training Cost Metrics

We found studies with potentially cost-saving screeners applied in the process of training SF candidates (Studies 3.5, 3.6, 3.7, and 3.13). We differentiated between 18X candidates and in-service candidates because training requirements differed substantially for these two paths to becoming SF.

We derived four factors relating to replacement cost per graduate: SFAS-specific 18X and in-service and whole-process 18X and in-service. As for cost factors that applied to all training, the basic inputs for each of the four factors are the cost of accession and the cost per graduate for certain types of courses, as well as the attrition rate for those courses. Also as before, building factors required taking into account not only the cost of the latest course but also the cost of previous courses taken, the attrition rates in those previous courses, and the cost of accession. Because of the numerous courses required for SF qualification and the substantial attrition in a number of them, the replacement cost for SFAS and SF graduates significantly exceeded the sum of the costs of accession and the cost of graduates from individual courses.

The details of the derivation of the four factors, as well as a metric for in-service accession, appear in the following sections.

Derivation of Replacement Costs for SFAS Graduates

The cost factors derived in this section are to be used for screeners that would be applied just before SFAS begins and for which the goal is to reduce the cost of a SFAS graduate.

18Xs

The cost of replacing a SFAS graduate who was an 18X is the cost per graduate of not only the SFAS course but also the cost of 2.2222 graduates of the Special Forces Preparation and Conditioning (SFPC) course, 2.5310 graduates from the Airborne course, etc. As shown in Table B.1, the number of graduates at each level takes into account course attrition rates. Note that we also established a factor of "proportion to replace" to recognize that most who fail to graduate in SFAS actually do not leave the Army. Thus, it is relatively rare that accession cost and 11B OSUT costs have to be reincurred due to a failure in SFAS.

Table B.1. Cost of Replacing an SFAS Graduate

Summary Cost Item	Cost per Graduate[a] (a)	Attrition Rate[a] (b)	Number to Replace (c)	Calculation of Number to Replace	Proportion to Replace (d)	Cost by Item (a) × (c) × (d)
Accession	$22,696	N/A	3.1678	2.8827 / (1 – 0.09)	0.16[b]	$11,503
11B OSUT	$27,775	9.0%	2.8827	2.5310 / (1 – 0.122)	0.16[b]	$12,811
Airborne	$9,124	12.2%	2.5310	2.2222 / (1 – 0.116)	1.0	$23,093
SFPC	$15,535	11.6%	2.2222	1.0000 / (1 – 0.55)	1.0	$34,522
SFAS	$20,229	55.0%	1.0000	N/A	1.0	$20,229
Total cost of replacement						$102,158

[a] From ATRM-159, TRADOC. *Attrition rates* are termed *p-factors* in ATRM-159.
[b] 11B OSUT FY 2012 graduates who had left the Army 3 years later (ATRRS, TAPDB).

In-Service Accessions

The calculation of the cost of replacing a SFAS graduate who was an in-service accession is parallel to the calculation for 18Xs, except that there is no prior training required because in-service accessions are recruited out of units (after their initial training is completed). Note also in the calculations in Table B.2 that the cost of accession is different because the process is completed in an entirely different way.

Table B.2. Cost of Replacing an In-Service Recruit SFAS Graduate

Summary Cost Item	Cost per Graduate	Attrition Rate[a]	Number to Replace (c)	Calculation of Number to Replace	Proportion to Replace (d)	Cost by Item (a) × (c) × (d)
In-service recruit	$8,423[a]	N/A	2.2222	1.0000 / (1 – 0.55)	1.0	$18,718
SFAS	$20,229[b]	55.0%[b]	1.0000	N/A	1.0	$20,229
Total cost of replacement						$38,947

[a] Derived from information from the SORB and RMC calculators. See derivation below.
[b] ATRM-159, TRADOC. What we call *attrition rates* here are termed *p-factors* in ATRM-159.

All SFAS Entrants

Once the individual cost factors were calculated, a combined figure had to be derived, as the research articles we dealt with did not typically give the breakout of 18X and in-service candidates in their samples. Working from unpublished 2015 RAND research, we estimated the proportion of course attendees from each source. Specifically, 54.2 percent of SFAS graduates were in-service and 45.8 percent were 18X candidates. Combining the figures earlier in that proportion gives a combined figure of \$67,898 (0.542 × \$38,947 + 0.458 × \$102,158). We adjusted this estimate by the inflation rate between September 2015 and September 2018 (1.0609), resulting in an FY 2018 cost of a replacement of \$72,033.

Cost of an In-Service Recruit

As detailed in Table B.3, the cost of an in-service recruit was derived from information provided by the SORB and from an RMC calculator available from the web. In-service recruits are accessed differently from those joining the military for the first time. An important part of the process involves SF recruiters assigned to the various regions with Army installations making visits to the installations to contact existing service members potentially interested in a SF career.

Table B.3. Operation Cost of SF Recruiting

Cost Item	Cost
Travel for procurement	\$1,323,576
Vehicles	\$250,992
Cell phones	\$86,310
Computers	\$37,400
Tablets	\$246,737
VAMP—SORB SF in-service marketing program	\$298,906
LAMP—SORB SF advertising	\$730,527
Total SF recruiting costs	\$3,074,448

SOURCE: Data provided by SORB.
NOTE: Based on 1,619 accessions and 125 recruiters. VAMP is a Management Decision Package that resources the Army marketing program, which is intended to inform the American people and motivate qualified candidates to consider Army service as soldiers or civilians. LAMP is the Local Advertising Management Program.

These figures assume 1,619 accessions and 125 SF recruiters. The average recruiter cost was calculated after determining (from TAPDB) that the average soldier in the position was an E-7 with 14 years of service, married, with two children. The average Army-wide RMC for such a person was determined to be about \$80,000 per year, which included an adjustment for housing cost for recruiters outside the continental United States (who generally do not receive a housing allowance as part of their pay). Table B.4 shows the estimated SF recruiting costs for in-service recruits.

Table B.4. SF Recruiting Costs per Accession

Cost Item	Cost	Source
a. Operational cost	$3,074,448	Table B.3
b. RMC for recruiters	$10,000,000	$80,000 × 125 recruiters
c. Incentive pay (79R recruiters Special Duty Pay for FY 2015)	$562,500	$375/month × 12 months × 125 recruiters (from SORB)
d. Total SF recruiting cost	$13,636,948	(a) + (b) + (c)
Total SF recruiting costs per accession	$8,423	(d) / 1,619 accessions

Derivation of Replacement Costs for Full SF Graduates

The cost factors derived in this section are to be used for screeners that would be applied on application for entry into SF and when the goal is to reduce the cost of a SF graduate.

18Xs

As shown in Table B.5, the derivation of the cost of replacing an 18X SF graduate parallels that for the cost of an SFAS graduate. The difference is that all SF qualification courses are considered, not just those through the SFAS course.

Table B.5. Cost of Replacing an 18X SF Graduate

Summary Cost Item	Cost per Graduate[a] (a)	Attrition Rate[a] (b)	Number to Replace (c)	Calculation of Number to Replace	Proportion to Replace (d)	Cost by Item (a) × (c) × (d)
Accession	$22,696	N/A	4.2872	3.9014 / (1 – 0.09)	0.16[b]	$15,568
11B OSUT	$27,775	9.0%	3.9014	3.4254 / (1 – 0.122)	0.16[b]	$17,338
Airborne	$9,124	12.2%	3.4254	3.0281 / (1 – 0.116)	1.0	$31,253
SFPC	$15,535	11.6%	3.0281	1.3626 / (1 – 0.55)	1.0	$47,041
SFAS	$20,229	55.0%	1.3626	1.2223 / (1 – 0.103)	1.0	$27,565
SFQC-orientation	$19,120	10.3%	1.2223	1.2088 / (1 – 0.011)	1.0	$23,370
SFQC-SERE	$10,065	1.1%	1.2088	1.1170 / (1 – 0.076)	1.0	$12,167
SFQC-SUT	$47,432	7.6%	1.1170	1.0946 / (1 – 0.02)	1.0	$52,980

Summary Cost Item	Cost per Graduate[a] (a)	Attrition Rate[a] (b)	Number to Replace (c)	Calculation of Number to Replace	Proportion to Replace (d)	Cost by Item (a) × (c) × (d)
SFQC-language (Arabic)	$121,421	2.0%	1.0946	1.0070 / (1 – 0.08)	1.0	$132,910
SFQC-MOS-engineer	$64,559	8.0%	1.0070	1.0000 / (1 – 0.007)	1.0	$65,014
SFQC-CULEX	$19,534	0.7%	1.0000	N/A	1.0	$19,534
Total cost of replacement						$444,739

NOTE: While there are a number of languages and MOS that candidates go into, we choose two specifics as examples. SFQC = Special Forces Qualification Course; SERE = survival, evasion, resistance, and escape; SUT = small unit training; and CULEX = culminating exercise.
[a] ATRM-159, TRADOC. *Attrition rates* are termed *p-factors* in ATRM-159.
[b] 11B OSUT FY 2012 graduates who had left the Army 3 years later (ATRRS, TAPDB).

In-Service Accessions

The derivation of the cost of replacing an in-service SF graduate parallels that for the cost of an SFAS graduate. As with those coming in through the 18X route, the difference is that all SF qualification courses are considered, not just those through the SFAS course, as shown in Table B.6. However, in-service candidates are recruited just before the SFAS course and, thus, take fewer courses to be SF qualified and do 18X candidates.

Table B.6. Cost of Replacing an In-Service SF Graduate

Summary Cost Item	Cost per Graduate[a] (a)	Attrition Rate[a] (b)	Number to Replace (c)	Calculation of Number to Replace	Proportion to Replace (d)	Cost by Item (a) × (c) × (d)
In-service recruit	$8,423[a]	N/A	3.0281	1.3626 / (1 – 0.55)	1.0	$25,505
SFAS	$20,229[b]	55.0%[b]	1.3626	1.2223 / (1 – 0.103)	1.0	$27,565
SFQC-orientation	$19,120	10.3%	1.2223	1.2088 / (1 – 0.011)	1.0	$23,370
SFQC-SERE	$10,065	1.1%	1.2088	1.1170 / (1 – 0.076%)	1.0	$12,167
SFQC-SUT	$47,432	7.6%	1.1170	1.0946 / (1 – 0.02)	1.0	$52,980
SFQC-language (Arabic)	$121,421	2.0%	1.0946	1.0070 / (1 – 0.08)	1.0	$132,910
SFQC-MOS-engineer	$64,559	8.0%	1.0070	1.0000 / (1 – 0.007)	1.0	$65,014
SFQC-CULEX	$19,534	0.7%	1.0000	N/A	1.0	$19,534
Total cost of replacement						$359,044

[a] Derived from information from the SORB and RMC calculators.
[b] ATRM-159, TRADOC. What are called *attrition rates* here are termed *p-factors* in ATRM-159.

Cost for All SF Entrants

After calculating the individual cost factors, we had to derive a combined figure. Working from unpublished 2015 RAND research, we estimated the proportion of course attendees who came from each source. Specifically, the group of SF graduates was shown to be 51.9 percent in-service and 48.1 percent 18X candidates. Combining these figures in that proportion gives a combined figure of $400,263 (0.519 times $359,044, plus 0.481 times $444,739). We adjusted this estimate by the inflation rate between September 2015 and September 2018 (1.0609), resulting in a FY 2018 cost of a replacement of $424,639.

Abbreviations

ABLE	Assessment of Background and Life Experiences
AC	Active Component
ACES	Army Continuing Education System
AFQT	Armed Forces Qualification Test
AFOQT	Air Force Officer Qualifying Test
AFOQT-PILOT	Air Force Officer Qualifying Test–Pilot
AFOQT-NAVT	Air Force Officer Qualifying Test–Navigator
AFSPP	U.S. Air Force Suicide Prevention Program
AIM	Assessment of Individual Motivation
AIT	Advanced Individual Training
APFT	Army Physical Fitness Test
APFTEP	Army Physical Fitness Test Enhancement Program
AQT	Aviation Qualification Test
ARI	U.S. Army Research Institute for the Behavioral and Social Sciences
ARMS	Assessment of Recruit Motivation and Strength
ASIP	Accession Screening and Immunization Program
ASVAB	Armed Services Vocational Aptitude Battery
ATRM	Army Training Resource Model
ATRRS	Army Training Requirements and Resources System
BCT	Basic Combat Training
CAI	Computer Assisted Instruction
CBT	Computer-Based Training
CULEX	culminating exercise
DA	Department of the Army
DEP	Delayed Entry Program
DRM	Dynamic Retention Model

EBF	exceeded body fat
EEEM	Expanded Enlistment Eligibility Metrics
EPAS	Enlisted Personnel Allocation System
FAP	Fitness Assessment Program
FAR	Flight Aptitude Rating
FAST	Functional Academic Skills Training
FY	fiscal year
G-1	Office of Deputy Chief of Staff for Personnel, U.S. Army
GED	General Educational Development
HQDA	Headquarters, Department of the Army
IET	Initial Entry Training
IPI	Inwald Personality Inventory
MAACL-R	Multiple Affect Adjective Check List–Revised
MMPI	Minnesota Multiphasic Personality Inventory
MOS	Military Occupational Specialty
MP	military police
MPA	Military Personnel Accessions
NEO-PI-R	NEO Personality Inventory–Revised
NLSI	Noncommissioned Officer Leadership Skills Inventory
NSF	Naval Special Forces (Norway)
NSG	nonstandardized group
OPTEMPO	operational tempo
OSUT	One Station Unit Training
PASS	positive affect and sensation-seeking
PPQ	Pilot Personality Questionnaire
PRT	Physical Readiness Training
PTRP	Physical Training and Rehabilitation Program
RBI	Rational Biodata Inventory
RMC	Regular Military Compensation

RRM	Recruiting Resource Model
SERE	survival, evasion, resistance, and escape
SF	Special Forces
SFAS	Special Forces Assessment and Selection
SFPC	Special Forces Preparation and Conditioning
SFQC	Special Forces Qualification Course
SG	standardized group
SORB	Special Operations Recruiting Battalion
SRB	Selective Reenlistment Bonus
SUPT	Specialized Undergraduate Pilot Training
SUT	small unit training
SWCS	Special Warfare Center and School
TA	Tuition Assistance
TAPAS	Tailored Adaptive Personality Assessment System
TAPDB	Total Army Personnel Data Base
TRADOC	U.S. Army Training and Doctrine Command
UBISS	Unit Based Injury Surveillance System
UNT	Undergraduate Navigator Training
UPT	Undergraduate Pilot Training
USAREC	U.S. Army Recruiting Command
USMEPCOM	U.S. Military Entrance Processing Command
VOLED	Voluntary Education
WQ	weight for height or body fat qualified
WPA	Work Preferences Assessment

References

Altarum, *Economic Analysis of Information Management Requirements, Injury Cause Coding*, 2006.

Anesgart, Martin N., and Joseph D. Callister, *Predicting Training Success with the NEO-PI-R: The Use of Logistic Regression to Determine the Odds of Completing a Pilot Screening Program*, Air Force Research Laboratory, Human Effectiveness Directorate, 2001.

Arth, Thomas O., Kurt W. Steuck, Christopher T. Sorrentino, and Eugene F. Burke, *Air Force Officer Qualifying Test (AFOQT): Predictors of Undergraduate Pilot Training and Undergraduate Navigator Training Success*, Air Force Human Resources Laboratory, 1990.

Asch, Beth J., James Hosek, Jennifer Kavanagh, and Michael G. Mattock, *Retention, Incentives, and DoD Experience Under the 40-Year Military Pay Table*, RAND Corporation, RR-1209-OSD, 2016. As of August 26, 2022:
https://www.rand.org/pubs/research_reports/RR1209.html

Asch, Beth J., James Hosek, and Michael G. Mattock, *Toward Meaningful Military Compensation Reform: Research in Support of DoD's Review*, RAND Corporation, RR-501-OSD, 2014. As of August 25, 2022:
https://www.rand.org/pubs/research_reports/RR501.html

Asch, Beth J., James Hosek, Michael Mattock, and Christina Panis, *Assessing Compensation Reform: Research in Support of the 10th Quadrennial Review of Military Compensation*, RAND Corporation, MG-764-OSD, 2008. As of August 16, 2022:
https://www.rand.org/pubs/monographs/MG764.html

Asch, Beth, Michael Mattock, and James Hosek, *How Do Federal Civilian Pay Freezes and Retirement Plan Changes Affect Employee Retention in the Department of Defense?* RAND Corporation, RR-678-OSD, 2014. As of August 25, 2022
https://www.rand.org/pubs/research_reports/RR678.html

Asch, Beth J., Michael G. Mattock, and James Hosek, *A New Tool for Assessing Workforce Management Policies Over Time: Extending the Dynamic Retention Model*, RAND Corporation, RR-113-OSD, 2013. As of August 25, 2022:
https://www.rand.org/pubs/research_reports/RR113.html

Bartone, Paul T., Robert R. Roland, James J. Picano, and Thomas J. Williams, "Psychological Hardiness Predicts Success in US Army Special Forces Candidates," *International Journal of Selection and Assessment*, Vol. 16, No. 1, 2008.

Beal, Scott A., *The Roles of Perseverance, Cognitive Ability, and Physical Fitness in U.S. Army Special Forces Assessment and Selection*, U.S. Army Research Institute, 2010.

Bedno, Sheryl A., David N. Cowan, Nadia Urban, and David W. Niebuhr, "Effect of Pre-Accession Physical Fitness on Training Injuries Among US Army Recruits," *Work*, Vol. 44, No. 4, 2013.

Boudreau, John W., "Effects of Employee Flows on Utility Analysis of Human Resource Productivity Improvement Programs," *Journal of Applied Psychology*, Vol. 68, No. 3, 1983.

Boudreau, John W., "Utility Analysis for Decisions in Human Resource Management," in Marvin D. Dunnette and Leaetta M. Hough, eds., *Handbook of Industrial and Organizational Psychology*, 2nd ed., Vol. 2, Consulting Psychologists Press, Inc., 1991.

Campbell, John P., and Lola M. Zook, *Building and Retaining the Career Force: New Procedures for Accessing and Assigning Army Enlisted Personnel—Final Report*, Human Resources Research Organization, 1996.

Carey, Neil, David Reese, and Robert Shuford, "Navy Self-Paced Computer-Based Courses: Practical Implications of Saving Time Under Instruction (UI)," *Military Psychology*, Vol. 22, No. 4, 2010.

Cascio, Wayne F., and Herman Aguinis, *Applied Psychology in Human Resource Management*, Pearson Education, 2011.

Castro, Carl Andrew, and Ann H. Huffman, *Predicting Retention Rates of U.S. Soldiers Stationed in Europe*, Army Medical Research Unit–Europe, 2002.

CNA, *Population Representation in the Military Services: Fiscal Year 2017 Summary Report*, Appendix B: *Active Component Enlisted Accessions*, Enlisted, 2017. https://www.cna.org/pop-rep/2017/

Cooke, Timothy W., and Aline O. Quester, "What Characterizes Successful Enlistees in the All-Volunteer Force: A Study of Male Recruits in the U.S. Navy," *Social Science Quarterly*, Vol. 73, No. 2, 1992.

Cornwell, Dan, *A Cost Benefit of Telemedicine: An Assessment of Aero-Medical Evacuation Patients Throughout the Pacific Basin*, Academy of Health Sciences (Army), Health Care Administration, 1995.

Cortina, Jose M., Mary L. Doherty, Neal Schmitt, Gary Kaufman, and Richard G. Smith, "The 'Big Five' Personality Factors in the IPI and MMPI: Predictors of Police Performance," *Personnel Psychology*, Vol. 45, No. 1, 1992.

Cowan, Douglas K., Linda E. Barrett, and Toni G. Wegner, *Air Force Officer Training School Selection System Validation*, Air Force Human Resources Lab, 1990.

DA—*See* Department of the Army.

Department of the Army, *Fiscal Year (FY) 2019 Budget Estimates*, Washington, D.C., 2018. As of March 15, 2021: https://www.asafm.army.mil/Portals/72/Documents/BudgetMaterial/2019/Base%20Budget/Operation%20and%20Maintenance/Army%20-%20Vol%201%20Justification%20Book.pdf

Fischl, M. A., and Deanne L. Blackwell, *Attrition in the Army from the Signing of the Enlistment Contract Through 180 Days of Service*, U.S. Army Research Institute for Behavioral and Social Sciences, 2000.

Garcia, Federico E., Ernest H. Joy, and David L. Reese, *Effectiveness of the Voluntary Education Program*, Center for Naval Analyses, 1998.

Granja-Alvarez, Juan Carlos, and Manuel José Barranco-García, "A Method for Estimating Maintenance Cost in a Software Project," *Software Maintenance Research and Practice*, Vol. 9, 1997.

Greenston, Peter M., *The Optimal Job-Person Match Case for Attrition Reduction*, U.S. Army Research Institute for the Behavioral and Social Sciences, 1997.

Hartmann, Ellen, and Cato Grønnerød, "Rorschach Variables and Big Five Scales as Predictors of Military Training Completion: A Replication Study of the Selection of Candidates to the Naval Special Forces in Norway," *Journal of Personality Assessment*, Vol. 91, No. 3, May 2009.

Hartmann, Ellen, Tor Sunde, Wenche Kristensen, and Monica Martinussen, "Psychological Measures as Predictors of Military Training Performance," *Journal of Personality Assessment*, Vol. 80, No. 1, March 2003.

Hauret, Keith G., Joseph J. Knapik, Jeffery L. Lange, Heidi A. Heckel, Dana L. Coval, and David H. Duplessis, "Outcomes of Fort Jackson's Physical Training and Rehabilitation Program in Army Basic Combat Training: Return to Training, Graduation, and 2-Year Retention," *Military Medicine*, Vol. 169, No. 7, July 2004.

Hauret, Keith G., Dana L. Shippey, and Joseph J. Knapik, "The Physical Training and Rehabilitation Program: Duration of Rehabilitation and Final Outcome of Injuries in Basic Combat Training," *Military Medicine*, Vol. 166, No. 9, 2001.

Holling, Heinz, "Utility Analysis of Personnel Selection: An Overview and Empirical Study Based on Objective Performance Measures," *Methods of Psychological Research*, Vol. 3, No. 1, January 1998.

Horgen, Kristen E., U. Christean Kubisiak, Valentina Bruk-Lee, Patrick W. Connell, Lisa M. Penney, Walter C. Borman, Victoria L. Pace, Elizabeth Lentz, Leonard A. White, Mark C. Young, and Stephen V. Bowles, *Evaluation and Refinement of a Screening Instrument for U.S. Army Recruiters: Noncommissioned Officer Leadership Skills Inventory*, U.S. Army Research Institute for the Behavioral and Social Sciences, March 2006.

Hwang, Jane S., Charles M. Lappan, Leonard C. Sperling, and Jon H. Meyerle, "Utilization of Telemedicine in the U.S. Military in a Deployed Setting," *Military Medicine*, Vol. 179, No. 11, 2014.

Johnson, Norman L., and Samuel Kotz, *Distributions in Statistics: Continuous Univariate Distribution*, Vol. 1, 1st ed., John Wiley & Sons, Inc., 1970.

Knapik, J. J., S. H. Bullock, S. Canada, E. Toney, J. D. Wells, E. Hoedebecke, and B. H. Jones, "Influence of an Injury Reduction Program on Injury and Fitness Outcomes Among Soldiers," *Injury Prevention*, Vol. 10, No. 1, February 2004.

Knapik, Joseph J., Salima Darakjy, Shawn Scott, Keith G. Hauret, Sara Canada, Roberto Marin, Frank Palkoska, Steven VanCamp, Eugene Piskator, William Rieger, and Bruce H. Jones, *Evaluation of Two Army Fitness Programs: The TRADOC Standardized Physical Training Program for Basic Combat Training and the Fitness Assessment Program*, Army Center for Health Promotion and Preventive Medicine, February 2004.

Knapik, J. J., K. Hauret, J. M. Bednarek, S. Arnold, M. Canham-Chervak, A. Mansfield, E. Hoedebecke, J. Mancuso, T. L. Barker, D. Duplessis, H. Heckel, J. Peterson, and the Staff of the US Army Physical Fitness School in the Year 2001, *The Victory Fitness Program: Influence of the US Army's Emerging Physical Readiness Training Doctrine on Fitness and Injuries in Basic Combat Training*, U.S. Army Center for Health Promotion and Preventive Medicine, July 2001.

Knapik, Joseph J., Keith G. Hauret, Jeffery L. Lange, and Brian Jovag, "Retention in Service of Recruits Assigned to the Army Physical Fitness Test Enhancement Program in Basic Combat Training," *Military Medicine*, Vol. 168, No. 6, June 2003.

Knapp, David, Beth J. Asch, Michael G. Mattock, and James Hosek, *An Enhanced Capability to Model How Compensation Policy Affects U.S. Department of Defense Civil Service Retention and Cost*, RAND Corporation, RR-1503-OSD, 2016. As of August 26, 2022: https://www.rand.org/pubs/research_reports/RR1503.html

Knapp, David, Bruce R. Orvis, Christopher Maerzluft, and Tiffany Berglund, *Resources Required to Meet Army's Enlisted Recruiting Requirements Under Alternative Recruiting Goals, Conditions, and Eligibility Policies*, RAND Corporation, RR-2364-A, 2018. As of August 16, 2022:
https://www.rand.org/pubs/research_reports/RR2364.html

Knapp, Deidre J., and Tonia S. Heffner, *Expanded Enlistment Eligibility Metrics (EEEM): Recommendations on a Non-Cognitive Screen for New Soldier Selection*, U.S. Army Research Institute for the Behavioral and Social Sciences, 2010.

Knapp, Deidre. J., and Kate A. LaPort, eds., *Tier One Performance Screen Initial Operational Test and Evaluation: 2012 Annual Report*, U.S. Army Research Institute for the Behavioral and Social Sciences, 2014.

Knapp, Deidre J., Kimberly S. Owens, and Matthew T. Allen, eds., *Validating Future Force Performance Measures (Army Class): In-Unit Performance Longitudinal Validation*, U.S. Army Research Institute for the Behavioral and Social Sciences, 2012.

Knox, Kerry L., Steven Pflanz, Gerald W. Talcott, Rick L. Campise, Jill E. Lavigne, Alina Bajorska, Xin Tu, and Eric D. Caine, "The US Air Force Suicide Prevention Program: Implications for Public Health Policy," *American Journal of Public Health*, Vol. 100, No. 12, 2010.

Korger, Chris, "The Road to Wings: How to Become a US Air Force Pilot—Part 1: An Overview," webpage, Fighter Sweep, 2019. As of August 25, 2022: https://fightersweep.com/262/how-to-become-a-us-air-force-pilot/

Larson, Gerald E., and Stephanie Booth Kewley, *First-Term Attrition in the Navy: Causes and Proposed Solutions*, Naval Health Research Center, 2000.

Lubin, Bernard, Edna R. Fielder, and Rodney Van Whitlock, "Predicting Discharge from Air Force Basic Training by Pattern of Affect," *Journal of Clinical Psychology*, Vol. 55, No. 1, January 1999.

Murphy, Kevin R., "When Your Top Choice Turns You Down: Effect of Rejected Offers on the Utility of Selection Tests," *Psychological Bulletin*, Vol. 99, No. 1, 1986.

Naval Inspector General, *Report to the Secretary of the Navy, Computer Based Training,* March 2009.

Niebuhr, David W., William F. Page, David N. Cowan, Nadia Urban, Marlene E. Gubata, and Patrick Richard, "Cost-Effectiveness Analysis of the U.S. Army Assessment of Recruit Motivation and Strength (ARMS) Program," Military Medicine, Vol. 178, No. 10, 2013.

Nock, Matthew K., Murray B. Stein, Steven G. Heeringa, Robert J. Ursano, Lisa J. Colpe, Carol S. Fullerton, Irving Hwang, James A. Naifeh, Nancy A. Sampson, Michael Schoenbaum, Alan M. Zaslavsky, and Ronald C. Kessler, "Prevalence and Correlates of Suicidal Behavior Among Soldiers: Results from the Army Study to Assess Risk and Resilience in Service Members (Army STARRS)," *JAMA Psychiatry*, Vol. 71, No. 5, May 2014.

Nye, Christopher D., Scott A. Beal, Fritz Drasgow, J. Douglas Dressel, Leonard A. White, and Stephen Stark, *Assessing the Tailored Adaptive Personality Assessment System*, U.S. Army Research Institute for the Behavioral and Social Sciences, 2014.

Nye, Christopher D., Fritz Drasgow, Oleksandr S. Chernyshenko, Stephen Stark, U. Christean Kubisiak, Leonard A. White, and Irwin Jose, *Assessing the Tailored Adaptive Personality Assessment System (TAPAS) as an MOS Qualification Instrument*, Personnel Decisions Research Institute (PDRI) Inc., 2012.

Office of the Under Secretary of Defense, Personnel and Readiness, *Population Representation in the Military Services: Fiscal Year 2017 Summary Report*, 2018. As of October 23, 2019: http://www.cna.org/research/pop-rep

Ohm, Diane, "Undergraduate Pilot/Navigator Training," webpage, Pittsburgh Air Reserve Station, January 27, 2009. As of August 25, 2022: https://www.pittsburgh.afrc.af.mil/News/Article-Display/Article/183953/undergraduate-pilotnavigator-training/

Orvis, Bruce R., Christopher E. Maerzluft, Sung-Bou Kim, Michael G. Shanley, and Heather Krull, *Prospective Outcome Assessment for Alternative Recruit Selection Policies*, RAND Corporation, RR-2267-A, 2018. As of August 26, 2022: https://www.rand.org/pubs/research_reports/RR2267.html

Public Law 115-232, National Defense Authorization Act for Fiscal Year 2019, August 13, 2018.

Putka, Dan J., and Kevin M. Bradley, *Relations Between Select21 Predictor Measures and First-Term Attrition*, Army Research Institute, 2008.

Rand, Elden R., Charles M. Lappan, Joseph C. Lee and James L. Furgerson, "Paging the Worldwide Cardiology Consultant: The Army Knowledge Online Telemedicine Consultation Program In Cardiology," *Military Medicine*, Vol. 174, No. 11, 2009.

Russell, Craig J., *Evidence-Based Human Resource Management*, Cognella Academic Publishing, 2016.

Santiago, Patcho N., Joshua E. Wilk, Charles S. Milliken, Carl A. Castro, Charles C. Engel, and Charles W. Hoge, "Screening for Alcohol Misuse and Alcohol-Related Behaviors Among Combat Veterans," *Psychiatric Services*, Vol. 61, No. 6, June 2010.

Schmeeckle, Joyce M., "Online Training: An Evaluation of the Effectiveness and Efficiency of Training Law Enforcement Personnel Over the Internet," *Journal of Science Education and Technology*, Vol. 12, No. 3, September 2003.

Shanley, Michael G., James C. Crowley, Matthew W. Lewis, Susan G. Straus, Kristin J. Leuschner, and John Coombs, *Making Improvements to the Army Distributed Learning Program*, RAND Corporation, MG-1016-A, 2012. As of August 30, 2022: https://www.rand.org/pubs/monographs/MG1016.html

Siem, Frederick M., "Predictive Validity of an Automated Personality Inventory for Air Force Pilot Selection," *International Journal of Aviation Psychology*, Vol. 2, No. 4, 1990.

Sticha, Paul J., Timothy A. Dall, Kristina Handy, Javier Espinosa, Paul. F. Hogan, and Mark C. Young, *Impact of the Army Continuing Education System (ACES) on Soldier Retention and Performance: Data Analyses*, U.S. Army Research Institute for the Behavioral and Social Sciences, 2003.

Street, D. R., Jr., K. T. Helton, and D. L. Dolgin, *The Unique Contribution of Selected Personality Tests to the Prediction of Success in Naval Pilot Training*, Naval Aerospace Medical Research Laboratory, 1992.

Strickland, William J., *A Longitudinal Examination of First Term Attrition and Reenlistment Among FY1999 Enlisted Accessions*, U.S. Army Research Institute for the Behavioral and Social Sciences, 2005.

Trent, L. K., "Evaluation of a Four- Versus Six-Week Length of Stay in the Navy's Alcohol Treatment Program," *Journal of Studies on Alcohol*, Vol. 59, No. 3, 1998.

Tzeng, Jeff, Christopher Jankosky, and Hayley Hughes, "Cost-Minimization Analysis of the U.S. Army Accession Screening and Immunization Program," *Military Medicine*, Vol. 177, No. 2, December 2012.

Vickers, Ross R., Jr., Linda K. Hervig, and Richard F. Booth, *Personality and Success Among Military Enlisted Personnel: An Historical Prospective Study of U.S. Navy Corpsmen*, Naval Health Research Center, 1996.

White, L. A., R. D. Nord, and F. A. Mael, *Setting Enlistment Standards on the ABLE to Reduce Attrition*, Army Research Institute, 1990.

Zook, Lola M., *Soldier Selection: Past, Present and Future*, Army Research Institute, 1996.

Made in United States
Troutdale, OR
09/16/2025

34584013R00073